THE MAHARISHI EFFECT

THE MAHARISHI EFFECT

A REVOLUTION THROUGH MEDITATION

ELAINE AND
ARTHUR ARON

STILLPOINT PUBLISHING
WALPOLE, NEW HAMPSHIRE
1986

FIRST PRINTING

Copyright © 1986 by Elaine and Arthur Aron. All rights reserved. No part of this book may be reproduced without written permission from the publisher, except by a reviewer who may quote brief passages or reproduce illustrations in a review; nor may any part of this book be reproduced, stored in a retrieval system, or transmitted in any form or by any means electronic, mechanical, photocopying, recording, or other, without written permission from the publisher.

This book is manufactured in the United States of America. It is designed by James F. Brisson, cover art by Tony Randazzo and published by Stillpoint Publishing, Box 640, Meetinghouse Road, Walpole, NH 03608.

Published simultaneously in Canada by Fitzhenry & Whiteside Limited, Toronto.

Library of Congress Card Catalog Number:
86-60445
Aron, Elaine and Arthur
The Maharishi Effect
ISBN 0-913299-26-X
0 9 8 7 6 5 4 3 2 1

*To the unbroken tradition
of enlightened teachers
who have preserved
this wisdom in
each generation.*

CONTENTS

INTRODUCTION — IX

1 WHAT'S GOING ON HERE?
Something Very Natural — 1

2 "WELL, MAYBE *INNER* PEACE IS POSSIBLE." — 17

3 THE BIG BREAKTHROUGH:
A Field Effect for Pure Consciousness — 37

4 THE GENTLE INVASION OF RHODE ISLAND — 55

5 HOW TO UNDERSTAND IT ALL:
Just Imagine a Bowling Ball... — 69

6 AND STILL BOLDER MOVES:
From Rhode Island to the World — 91

7 STILL MORE EVIDENCE — 109

8 IF THE QUESTION OF CAUSALITY STILL LINGERS — 121

9 A WORLD OF DIFFERENCE — 135

10 WHAT IF IT'S ALL TRUE? — 153

REFERENCES — 161

INDEX — 175

INTRODUCTION

You have picked up a book about a discovery that is going to change the world. It will maintain world peace, and it will do much, much more.

Let's start, however, with keeping the peace — that would be impressive enough, and the prerequisite to any further accomplishments on earth. Every minute of every day, weapons are poised, and all humans remotely able to make them fire must be thinking clearly or life on earth ends. The problem is simple.

The solutions have not been. It is frightening to know that, in spite of many fine words and deeds in the name of peace, humans have regularly gone to war — or fired their weapons by accident. Obviously our usual ways of preventing violence, war and accidents have not worked. Something different is needed. Or as the farmers put it, "For a new crop, sow a new seed."

By definition, new seeds are not familiar, not yet totally acceptable. Still, when the old crop threatens to fail, it is blind, stubborn ignorance not to test a new seed and see what it can do. While the

approach examined in this book is certainly not familiar, its advantages are simply too impressive to ignore:
1. It is entirely grassroots — governments need not be involved.
2. It asks no sacrifices of anyone — people participate eagerly because it directly improves their individual lives.
3. Even then, only a small percentage of the population is needed in order to influence the whole globe.
4. None of those involved need to believe or even know that what they are doing affects the world — skeptics are equally effective.
5. Nor does it even nudge the world in the direction of any specific ideology. The best theories about it suggest that it does its job merely by greatly increasing the coherence of human thought.
6. Amazing as it all sounds, this approach is not mystical. Science discovered it and has throughly researched it. Indeed, it is one of the few approaches to peace that is even capable of being studied scientifically.

We are keenly aware of how difficult it is to believe that the complexities of international conflict have a simple solution. For the cause of peace, some of you have lobbied, boycotted, marched, prayed, sung, donated, signed petitions, and burned porch lights — all with uncertain results at best. It would be surprising if you were not cynical about a "new seed."

All we ask, however, is that you read what we have to say — even miracle hybrids must first be sown. In particular, we are not asking you to take anything between these covers on faith. This book is not about theory or personal experience. It is about hard data. Indeed, it is the theory that you may find most difficult to accept. The research results — the facts — are extremely convincing. As professional researchers ourselves, we have pored over these studies in detail, and we are confident that they were designed carefully and carried out properly. The data are solid.

Of course, data can be boring. Thus we have tried to make this book entertaining too, telling you the story of the people and events that made the discovery possible. But the main entertainment is going to be the exhilaration of a world-changing vision of what human minds can do.

Elaine and Art Aron
Capitola, CA
Feburary, 1986

THE MAHARISHI EFFECT

1

What's Going On Here? Something Very Natural

It was 1978, in the midst of the Iranian revolution. In the alley behind one of Tehran's major hotels, thousands of people were jammed — shouting, honking horns, throwing rocks. Inches away on the other side of a wall, in a meeting room in the hotel, there was a profound silence. Thirty men sat comfortably in chairs, their eyes closed and their faces relaxed and serene. They were of different races, nationalities and ages, but right then they all gave the same comforting impression of an indescribable inner beauty.

These men happened to be meditating. They had no monopoly on inner grace, of course. You've probably seen a similar look on the face of a child, a person deep in prayer, an artist creating, or any one of us when exalting over a new insight perhaps, or a new baby, or the view from a cliff beside the sea. It's a natural expression for our species, even if too rare.

But these men were meditating for a special reason: they had come to Iran to try to make social changes take place there as peacefully as possible. They didn't care which side won — that was the Iranians' business. They simply wanted to save lives and turmoil, and they wanted to see if meditating in a group would help.

On that evening, as one of them told us later, "It was actually one of the best meditations I'd ever had. It was like that for a lot of us." But the hotel manager was in quite another state and rushed in towards evening to insist that these quiet guests pack up along with the others and be ready to move. "This place," he shouted, "is going to be burned to the ground!"

The hotel manager was partly right — every other foreign-owned hotel in the area was looted or burned that day. Every one but this one.

For three months, groups of meditators as small as thirty and as large as two hundred stayed in Tehran. They rarely left their hotels and had almost no contact with the Iranians. But if shooting erupted near their hotel, they meditated, and the shooting stopped. If violence flared in any of the smaller Iranian cities, a delegation was sent to meditate there — just meditate — and the violence immediately subsided. Every time.

Muharram, a major holiday celebrated by millions, was predicted by the press to be a "certain bloodbath." But the meditating group was there and it was peaceful. Again, the meditators did not care which side won. They were operating on a very special theory: *if a large enough group of people — and they had a formula for estimating the number — were all drawing on the calm, coherence, and wisdom deep within the silent human mind, then those qualities would prevail in the environment and the right changes, whatever they were, would come about.*

In the case of Iran, the organization sponsoring the experiment was never able to bring in enough people — and then the visas of those in Iran ran out and could not be renewed. We all know the story since. But this is only one instance of many similar attempts, and this book will describe every one that we know about

— especially those that have been studied scientifically, since we are social scientists and prefer our evidence in a scientific package. (The stories in this book are all true, although minor details such as people's names may have been changed.) But perhaps you have your own stories of inner peace stemming the tides of violence. Certainly these thirty men who went to Iran do. Now returned to their various occupations, they still talk about it, still feel Iran could be at peace again, if only they could go back . . . or if only enough Iranians . . .

The Experience of Pure Consciousness

What were those few men doing that could have had such an effect on the entire nation of Iran?

Like other courageous souls in history, they were "waging peace" with the newest yet oldest weapon of peace. It has many different names, but we will call it the "experience of pure consciousness."

This experience is new in that it has been scientifically studied for only about fifteen years and experimentally applied to the problem of war, violence and social incoherence for only the last ten. But after these few years of research, we now know that while these men were meditating in their Tehran hotel, their breathing had probably essentially stopped several times; their metabolic rate had decreased twice as much as during the deepest stage of sleep; and an electroencephalogram (EEG) of their brain waves would have indicated nearly complete coherence of neural activity in the brain — something seen at no other time in adult humans. (We will describe this body of research in more detail in Chapter 2.)

All these changes indicate a depth of physical rest never observed before by physiologists. Yet if asked, these thirty men would have said they felt not drowsy or semi-conscious but fully alert and aware. Not aware of any particular thoughts, perceptions or feelings, however, but aware of their own consciousness, by itself. Free and pure. Described with words like "unbounded," "whole" or "perfectly silent."

If the physiological description of what they were doing was new, the experience itself was very old. At least since the beginning of human records, men and women in almost every culture and generation have described "pure consciousness"— "*samadhi*" (ancient India), "*nirvana*" (Buddha), "the oceanic experience" (Freud), "the vision of the form of the Good" (Plato), the "Pure Contemplation of the One" (early Greek Christians), the "Naught" or "Divine Nothingness" (Hasidic Jews). In the Jewish-Hasidic and Christian-monastic traditions, descriptions of pure consciousness recognize prayer as a first step in the process. In the last stage there are no thoughts or feelings — just perfect awareness or love or union with God. The descriptions are numerous and beautiful — we highly recommend reading one of the many anthologies of "mystical writings" in your own tradition in order to appreciate the universality of the pure consciousness experience. While we can't go back and compare the effects of today's meditation to the physiological state of those in the past, those descriptions that have survived seem almost as precise — and certainly more poetic than the physiologists'! The following are examples taken from Brett's *History of Psychology*.[1]

Philo, a Jewish philosopher born around 20 B.C., said, "Therefore if any desire come upon thee, O soul, to be the inheritor of the good things of God, leave not only thy country, thy body, and thy kindred, thy outward sense, and thy father's house, that is speech, but also flee from thyself and depart out of thy self" for the "enjoyment of light, a most penetrating sight, a most manifest energy . . . Divine Illumination."

In Egypt in the third century, Plotinus stated that "in this contemplation of the eternal, the soul comes to rest and does not move out of itself as it does in reflection." To Plotinus it was "the final and best state of the soul, its final and complete unity."

In the fifth century St. Augustine claimed "We, raising up ourselves with a more flowing affection toward the 'self-same,' did by degrees pass through all things bodily . . . and we came to our own minds and went beyond them, that we might arrive at the region of never-failing plenty, where Thou feedest Israel forever with the food of truth." Brett explains that "the terms self, knowledge and life were fundamentally one . . . behind them all is consciousness, in which the self is one with itself . . . The soul discovers itself and its own nature, reveals itself to itself and understands that its content is no other than itself expanded."

In the autobiography written at the command of her confessors to give a precise account of her unusual experiences, St. Teresa of sixteenth-century Spain provided a vivid account of some of the physiological effects of meditation. "All the faculties now fail and are suspended in such a way that, as I have said, it is impossible to believe they are active. If the soul has been meditating on a subject, this vanishes from its memory as if it had never thought of it . . . While seeking God in this way, the soul becomes conscious that it is fainting, completely away, in a kind of swoon, with an exceeding great and sweet delight. It gradually ceases to breathe and all its bodily strength begins to fail."[2]

Patanjali of ancient India wrote, "When . . . there are no more thought waves at all in mind, then one enters the *samadhi* which is called 'seedless'."[3]

On the other side of the globe, Lame Deer of the Sioux nation describes the experience in his tradition:

> The *wicasa wakan* [a type of medicine man] wants to be by himself . . . he likes to meditate . . . [he] loves silence, wrapping it around himself like a blanket — a loud silence with a voice like thunder tells him many things . . . from all living beings something flows into him all the time, and something flows from him. I don't know where or what, but it's there. I know. This kind of medicine man is neither good nor bad. He lives — and that's it, that's enough.[4]

A North American meditator in the 1970s said, "It is like skiing down a ski jump; at a certain point you leave the ski jump and suddenly you are in the air. In transcending, you dive down and down, then 'click,' you find yourself in that other state, just 'there'."[5]

The ability to transcend seems to be natural to the human race as a whole. Yet it has also been rare, in spite of efforts by most of those who have stumbled upon the experience to share it. Apparently the phenomenon was too scattered and too poorly understood ever to achieve the necessary critical mass of those experiencing it, teaching it, and talking about it, which could have then made the experience available to others.

However, in the last twenty-five years all this has changed. Such a critical mass has developed; it is obvious throughout our culture. Along with it has come a very detailed scientific understanding of the experience and its potential. This research seems to validate the significance the experience has always been granted in every society. In particular, it has been nourished and treasured not only as a profound personal experience, but as a means (often the only means) to guide the individual and the community up out of pettiness, confusion, and violence. Now a substantial body of recent research indicates that the experience of pure consciousness can (a) eradicate much of the violence and disharmony among humans, including war, and (b) increase intelligence, creativity, and longevity to levels beyond current limits. This discovery (or rather, rediscovery) appears to be *the single most important scientific achievement of our time — one that might keep us from destroying ourselves and our planet.*

That's an enormous claim. But before you scoff, think about it. What if it's true?

The Scientific Study of Pure Consciousness
First, a Word About This Book's Approach

The increase in the last twenty-five years in the interest in the experience of pure consciousness has taken many forms. But this book relies mainly on the research on the Transcendental Meditation or "TM" technique as taught by Maharishi Mahesh Yogi. Of course, the experience of pure consciousness is at least as old as the human nervous system, whereas the name "TM" is as old as 1958! But there are two reasons for this emphasis.

First, the scientific study of the pure consciousness experience has been done almost exclusively with individuals practicing this particular form of meditation. Science needs consistency in procedures, and the TM technique is taught the same way to everyone who practices it, by identically trained teachers who teach a highly systematic twelve-hour course. Most other forms of meditation available in the West have been developed independently or taught by books, which each reader may understand differently. Either way, results are variable. However, with the TM program, scientists in London or Denver can compare results with their colleagues in Amsterdam or Mexico City and know they are studying the same phenomenon. They also have large numbers to work with, allowing them to compare averages. Two or three million have been taught the TM technique worldwide, so research subjects are always available.

Also, science needs to study a phenomenon in the simplest, purest form available. Often meditation instruction is mixed in with advice about lifestyle, diet, personal conduct, or philosophy. All these could affect physiological or psychological measures, so that any research done would be on more than simply the experience of pure consciousness. In contrast, the TM course does not advise or require the adoption of any other behaviors or attitudes — it simply teaches what to do to have that single experience consistently.

But the second and main reason for our emphasis on the TM technique is that it does definitely produce the pure consciousness experience. This is clear from the research and from the close parallels between reports of TM meditators and most pre-science descriptions of the experience. While the term "TM" is relatively young, it comes from the oldest known source of knowledge about meditation and pure consciousness, the Vedic tradition of India. This consistency makes it much easier for researchers to be confident that when people close their eyes intending to have this experience, they actually do.

In conclusion, it is possible that other meditation techniques give rise to similar experiences (although many clearly don't).[6] But they can't be very useful for the purposes of scientific research if they aren't widely practiced, uniformly taught, or likely to produce the experience consistently.

We want to emphasize, however, that our focus on TM research to understand pure consciousness and its effects does not make this a "TM book." Rather, it is a book on pure consciousness — for all those interested in that experience, or in any aspect of human consciousness, or in world peace, or simply in the human species.

Now a word for those of you who doubt the experience of pure consciousness even exists, regardless of what technique people use to try to attain it. Some of you may have picked up this book out of curiosity seasoned with a dash of doubt, and you're saying, "They probably meditate, so the book is bound to be full of biases, distortions, and wishful thinking. To study something as subjective as 'pure consciousness,' the investigators should at least be disinterested."

It's true — we've been using the TM technique for fourteen years. But that does not disqualify us, as sociologists of science will tell you.[7] In fact, generally scientists who care passionately about a subject — be it evolution, the unconscious, or relativity — create the lasting theories and do the pioneering research. Of course, the methods and traditions of science do help keep these pioneers fairly objective. And later, after they have had their say, other disinterested scientists (who may have passionate interests of their own in other areas of science) tidy up the details and correct any wild shots. So it is scientifically safe that we do care very much about the contents of this book. If we didn't care about it, we wouldn't have written it — or sacrificed comfortable careers to pursue the sometimes academically isolated directions in which it has led.

Nevertheless, we *are* scientists. This means among other things that in this book we have avoided discussing techniques or experiments that have not been evaluated with the traditional scientific methods of objective, repeatable measurements that control as much as possible for alternative hypotheses.

The purpose of all these cautions is to warn that this book may require some patience on almost everyone's part. It may be too scientific for our "new age consciousness" friends and too far outside the current scientific paradigm for many of our social science friends. But we could see no other honest way to write it. We hope you understand.

Four Findings About Pure Consciousness

This book explores four major findings about the experience of pure consciousness (focusing mainly on the third).

1. **The dramatic physiological changes during the experience of pure consciousness.** We've seen that these have been described repeatedly in nonscientific but consistent terms by isolated individuals throughout history. But their **scientific** delineation probably began in 1970, with the work of Robert "Keith" Wallace at U.C.L.A. Before his work, scattered studies of yogis and Zen monks were in the research literature, but the results were difficult to generalize beyond these unique subjects. Wallace's research on TM meditators marked the beginning of an explosion of studies, especially after Wallace concluded he was studying "a fourth major state of consciousness [besides sleeping, dreaming and ordinary wakefulness] that is physiologically and biochemically quite unique."[8]

   After fifteen years of scientific activity, a quite detailed picture of the physiology of pure consciousness has emerged. Chapter 2 describes these physiological effects briefly.

2. **The experience's ability to remove the effects of stress from the body, increase longevity, and improve human functioning.** Scientific work on the possible long-term benefits of the experience also began in the early seventies. Stress expert Hans Selye pointed out that the physiological effects seen in Wallace's research were the exact opposite of those caused by stress.[9] Selye, and others since, have amply demonstrated that stress is the fundamental cause of almost all human health problems. Thus researchers such as Keith Wallace, David Orme-Johnson[10] (then at the University of Texas), and many others began looking at meditators' mental and physical health. They found that the pure consciousness experience enhances a person's resistance to and recovery from stress.

This research on the long-term benefits of the pure consciousness experience has now extended well beyond health issues, to include over three hundred studies from around the world on all aspects of human functioning, from academic performance to susceptibility to perceptual illusions, from marital happiness to moral judgment — anything that might benefit from the nervous system being rested and functioning coherently. Perhaps the most interesting research is still being done by Keith Wallace — on signs of increased longevity in TM meditators.[11]

The findings from all these investigations are also reviewed in Chapter 2, speedily and without jargon. Our purpose is to show you why it is reasonable to consider this experience to be real and powerful, as a basis for exploring the next point.

3. **Solely by having this experience, an individual finds that the social environment becomes more coherent and harmonious.** This effect was first demonstrated scientifically in a study by the sociologist Garland Landrith in 1974.[12] By 1978 it looked

What's going on here? 11

almost irrefutable, and we started planning this book. Beginning with Chapter 3, each adds additional support for this point, in the same order as the research has been done. In fact, as we were writing this book, every few months we had to add a new chapter or condense the others because the research literature is growing so fast. There is a great deal of evidence for this unusual idea, which has come to be called the "Maharishi Effect," after the originator of the technique that made possible the research on and widespread application of this ancient idea.

4. **All of the above is possible because the pure consciousness experience is actually the subjective experience of what in physics is called the "unified field."** An understanding that the pure consciousness experience is an experience of some type of universal field has seemed intuitively obvious to virtually all who have described the experience, from Plato to Carl Jung. But its scientific confirmation has had to wait for a number of events: a large and varied population having the experience, a clear theory of the consequences of such an interpretation of the experience, scientific methods of studying the predictions arising from that interpretation, and positive results from such studies.

All these were available by the late seventies, yet still it was difficult to conceptualize this "universal field of consciousness." It was all too amazing. Then, in 1983, physicists developed the first really workable unified field theory for the physical world. A unified field has been the goal of physics since Einstein. Finally, in the 1980s, it is taking shape. And the beauty of it is that it is not a "physical" field at all, in the "material" sense of the word. Rather, it seems to express in the terms of modern science, the equations of quantum physics, the exact field described for thousands of years in more subjective terms by those experiencing pure consciousness.

What is this field, in plain English? A universal field in which the four force fields (gravitational, electromagnetic, and weak- and strong-nuclear), plus the basic particle fields that constitute the physical world, all exist in an undifferentiated, non-material, yet real, state. The unified field is thought to have been the only field at the moment of the "big bang" when the universe began. Now it exists simultaneously with its manifestations. According to quantum physics, by virtue of this non-material unified field *acting upon itself*, forces and particles exist and give rise to our concrete, visible universe (much as undifferentiated consciousness gives rise to specific thoughts).

This point is discussed in Chapter 5 (along with other possible explanations for the research findings we describe in this book).

How We Suggest You Take This Book

We have made a whopping claim — that in this book we are describing what may be the most important scientific discovery of our time. We can't expect many of you to believe that yet. But we do expect you to approach this book with an open mind.

A Short Course in Open-Mindedness

In science, an open mind is the most essential tool. In fact, whatever their personal prejudices, good scientists consider nothing definitely proven or disproven. Everything is figured in probabilities — even that the sun will rise tomorrow. Of course, based on statistical probabilities about the sun's past behavior, scientists might call it a good bet! That is, they have a "good theory" about the sun, the orbits of the planets, and gravity generally. As scientists, however, they are never sure. They realize they could have made one of two kinds of errors.

"Type I" errors occur when we accept something to be true

when it really is not — agree that the sun *always* rises, and then find one day it doesn't. And "Type II" errors occur when we accept something to be untrue when it actually is true — announce the sun does not always rise and then end up feeling a little foolish every morning.

Type I errors are feared most by "pure science" because whole theories could be built up on phenomena thought to be true that aren't. Therefore, all research results — especially results that appear to support a new theory — are put through rigorous statistical and logical analyses to be very sure they didn't occur by chance or because of some cause other than what the theory proposed.

Type II errors are most feared by those testing practical solutions to problems, such as a new treatment. Researchers do not want to decide something does not work and discourage all further research on that treatment when it actually does work. (Of course, if there is a possibility of dangerous side effects, a Type I error is equally feared.)

In this light, we could argue that the research results described in this book — on a simple solution to the world's most pressing problems — ought to be viewed with great leniency, for fear of making a Type II error. After all, the pure consciousness experience not only has no adverse side effects but appears to be very beneficial to individuals, whatever its social influence. If it doesn't turn out to work in the larger context, nothing would be lost.

In reality, however, the research results described in this book have not received such generous treatment.

Nor have these results usually needed it. They are solid. Subjected to the most rigorous standards of Type-I-error avoidance, they have survived fine. As one independent criminologist said after reviewing one of the studies for the *St. Petersburg Times*, "the paper was absolutely beyond fault in terms of research design. It was impeccable."[13]

But the Real Problem Is "How Could It Be?"

If the research is so solid, you probably wonder why this new "treatment" remains largely unused. Because the same criminologist quoted above — just as an example — after calling this research "impeccable," said in his next breath, "But I don't believe it. There is no explanation in current scientific thought that would explain this phenomenon."

Of course there is an explanation — our Point 4 (pure consciousness as an experience of the unified field), which we discuss in Chapter 5. But the concept is difficult for most of us to accept. The universal unified field which must be posited in order to explain the field effects of pure consciousness is not something we can directly see, touch, taste, smell, or hear. We need to realize that the field's invisibility does not mean that we must accept its existence on faith. Few frontiers of modern science are directly accessible to our senses; we've finished exploring what's close or on the surface. But these invisible phenomena can still be objectively verified. They can also yield powerful, highly visible technologies.

However, most of us are behind the times. We experience and believe in a physical world that obeys the "classical" laws of physics, the ones we can personally observe — like "what goes up must come down." These principles are true at the level humans perceive with their unaided senses. In fact, the laws looked so true that physicists at the turn of the century thought they had discovered all there was to know about the physical world. Just a few details needed to be filled in.

Their complacency was shattered by the discovery of little oddities like radioactivity and relativity. Soon it was found that at the extremes of creation — the level of the atomic nucleus and of the galaxies — the laws of classical physics were violated so frequently that an entirely new understanding of reality had to be evolved. Matter and energy were no longer fundamental. Fields were fundamental. On the basis of field theories, the laws of relativity and quantum mechanics were born, with improbable concepts like time-space geometry, superfluidity, perpetual motion and, most recently, the unified field.

It is not that it is impossible for anyone but a physicist to conceive of a "non-classical" physical world made up of nonmaterial quantum fields. For example, although we have never tasted, touched, or otherwise experienced radioactivity (a product of quantum fields), we believe it exists. We know it has crucial effects, though these are invisible and may not manifest themselves for years. In part, we decide to know because a Type II error about radioactivity (saying it doesn't exist when it does) risks our survival. Perhaps the field effects of pure consciousness could have similar, though opposite, survival value!

Where Are the Social Sciences in All This?

The social sciences are still back at the point physics was at when it realized its classical laws would not suffice. Complacency is gone. Although many isolated facts about human behavior have been discovered, our understanding as a whole is still a hopeless muddle. But unlike physics, the social sciences have not seen any way out of their muddle. Could the reason be that social scientists have so far failed to look for any interaction between human behavior and those subatomic phenomena that led to quantum-field physics? After all, a unified field must include humans too.

Of course, physicists have not seen much connection either between the unified field and other human concerns like crime and love and auto accidents and world peace. But this book says there is a connection. In fact, we predict it will become utterly obvious to everyone by the next century. But we only ask you to consider the possibility without prejudgment. We'll provide the evidence, you provide the open mind. That's all that will be required; the research described in this book speaks well for itself.

The Organization of This Book

This chapter has introduced the book's main themes. The next chapter discusses our Points 1 and 2 — the research on what happens to the individual during and as a result of the pure consciousness experience. Then, once the nature of the experience is clear, Chapter 3 begins to look at the scientific evidence for Point 3 by describing the first studies that linked the presence of small percentages of meditators in cities with declines in crime rates.

Chapter 4 describes an experiment involving the entire state of Rhode Island. Chapter 5 looks at the explanations for these various results, especially explanations from quantum physics — our Point 4. Chapter 6 takes up the experiment that produced the events in Iran described at the start of this chapter. This experiment applied the field effect of pure consciousness to five world trouble-spots during the fall of 1978. Chapter 7 describes subsequent applications in the territory of Delhi, India; Puerto Rico; and Holland.

Chapter 8 explores two studies done in Israel and Washington, D. C., which were especially designed to settle the question of causality. That is, they finish the job of demonstrating that people experiencing pure consciousness really *cause* the changes in crime rate, violence, auto accidents, suicides, and so forth that have been associated with higher numbers of individuals experiencing pure consciousness in an area.

Chapter 9 describes the most recent results, from experiments with 1,600 and 7,000 persons experiencing pure consciousness together — the numbers predicted to be enough to affect the U. S. and the world, respectively. In both cases the results were dramatic. Finally, Chapter 10 asks you to consider, "What does it all mean?"

2

"Well, Maybe *Inner* Peace Is Possible."

Eric's screaming. He screams every night at this hour, just when Maryanne is trying to cook dinner, talk with Paul about his day, and report on or forget about her own frustrations. Being a one-year-old, Eric does not realize he is helping to drive his parents to the brink of divorce. But to Paul and Maryanne, this baby has become the last straw. Who knew family life would be so difficult?

Two weeks later, Eric is playing quietly, his stomach full and bedtime on his mind. Paul watches him while setting the table. In the other room, Maryanne is sitting on the bed, her eyes are closed, her thoughts of Eric and Paul and responsibilities are temporarily gone. Last week she learned to meditate. She does it regularly now, morning and evening. If we could measure what's happening to her physiologically at the moment, we'd find her heart rate is very low, her breathing shallow, and throughout her body biochemical changes are happening that indicate deep rest and major repair work going on. But her slight, relaxed smile could tell us more.

When she's done, it will be Paul's turn. Then they'll put Eric to bed, have dinner and enjoy the evening together. Who knew family life would be so nice?

Maryanne and Paul have simply found that experiencing pure consciousness is a pleasant, easy, and effective way to feel better at the start and again near the end of each day. But in the past, the experience has seemed dramatic, even startling to people. One brief experience has often caused people to change the whole course of their lives — to write books about pure consciousness (Richard Bucke[1]), to try to prove its existence scientifically (Carl Jung[2], Gustav Fechner[3j]), and generally to try to enlighten the rest of the world (St. Augustine, St. Teresa). No doubt this was because the experience constrasted so much with everyday life, and because it was just so unexpected. It can be dramatic today too, but less so when the experience is understood and expected, comes on very gently and naturally, and increases gradually with each day.

But let's not be so impersonal. Suppose *you* are experiencing pure consciousness. Let's say you have taken a TM course.* Now you have just closed your eyes to meditate. Immediately you notice you feel quieter, calmer, and more relaxed. Mental activity settles down and physical activity settles down — like two legs of a table, they go together. You begin to think to yourself the sound you were given, chosen by your instructor because "it has a vibrational quality known from tradition to suit your particular type of nervous system." And you continue to think it, in the specific way you were taught, without forcing or concentrating. You feel

---

*The TM course is described in several excellent books: H. H. Bloomfield, M. P Cain, and D. T. Jaffe, *TM: Discovering Inner Energy and Overcoming Stress* (New York: Delacorte, 1975); D. Denniston and P. McWilliams, *The TM Book* (New York: Warner Books, 1975); and J. Forem, *Transcendental Meditation* (New York: Dutton, 1973).

still more settled. Thoughts come. And go. Soon your breathing becomes very light. You are vaguely aware of a dog barking across the street. You wonder what you'll have for dinner. But you keep going deeper, always deeper.

The sound you've been gently repeating gets so quiet, so subtle . . . and then it's just gone. Thoughts are gone too. There's only silence. A sense of wholeness. Unboundedness. Perhaps it only lasts a fleeting moment, perhaps it lasts several minutes. Perhaps when it comes again, thoughts occur along with it, so that the sense of silence and unboundedness is more like a background to thoughts and perceptions, a screen on which they play, a pond across which they ripple . . .

But as the minutes pass, the experience keeps returning, whether clear and isolated or vague and mixed. Sometimes it almost seems to push out your day's concerns and replace them with — strange as it seems — a deep happiness.

And then you glance at your watch and twenty minutes are up, "right on the button." You spend a few minutes coming out of that state. And then you're off to a busy day or evening, feeling alert, enthusiastic, energized yet relaxed.

Research on What Happens to the Body During the Pure Consciousness Experience

That's how the experience feels to a meditator. How does it look to a physiologist?

People's experiences vary — from day to day and from each other's. Every nervous system is different and constantly changing. But research has found that the general physiological effects are quite uniform.

Most studies are of the pattern of physiological functioning during the overall TM meditation period, without regard to moment-to-moment changes in the experience. These studies are summarized in Table 1.

TABLE 1

TYPICAL PHYSIOLOGICAL CHANGES OBSERVED DURING TM® MEDITATION

Reduced metabolic rate [4, 5, 6, 7]

Decreased breath volume [8]

Reduced heart rate [5, 9]

Increased blood flow to the brain [10]

Increased skin resistance (a measure of relaxation) [7, 11, 12, 13]

Increased muscle relaxation [14]

Reduced blood lactate (a biochemical indicator of stress) [7, 15]

Reduced plasma cortisol (a major stress hormone) [16, 17]

Reduced noradrenaline metabolite (indicating lower physiological arousal) [18]

Increased serotonin metabolite (indicating rest and relaxation) [18]

Increased synchronization and coherence of the EEG ("brain waves") [19, 20, 21, 22, 23, 24]

Isolating the specific effects of meditation's deepest phase, the pure consciousness experience, is trickier — its exact onset, duration, and other qualities are much harder to observe. This is why Table 2, which lists research of this kind, is much shorter than Table 1.

TABLE 2

PHYSIOLOGICAL CHANGES FOUND TO OCCUR DURING THE PURE CONSCIOUSNESS EXPERIENCE SPECIFICALLY
(from Research Conducted Thus Far)

Breathing nearly stops [8, 25]
Heart rate drops dramatically [8, 25, 26]
Skin resistance (a measure of relaxation) increases greatly [8, 25]
EEG becomes almost perfectly coherent [8, 25, 26, 27]

It's usually assumed that studying the overall period of meditation, which is typically about twenty minutes and usually includes some experiences of pure consciousness, approximates studying the experience itself, which is briefer but more intense. Certainly for practical purposes the distinction is not very important. Still, it is interesting to try to isolate the physiological pattern associated specifically with the pure consciousness experience.

This task was first accomplished by physiologist John Farrow [8, 25], who used an ingenious experimental procedure to conduct research involving 125 TM meditators in the United States and Europe. He had his research subjects meditate while hooked up to all sorts of apparatus, and, on top of that, had them press a button during their meditation whenever they had just finished an experience of pure consciousness.

Pure consciousness must be a fairly resilient experience, because Farrow's research subjects managed to press the button — often several times in a single twenty-minute meditation. And he found that on those physiological activities he was monitoring, the usual changes associated with the overall TM-meditation period were greatly magnified just before the button press (the period when his subjects were experiencing pure consciousness). As seen in Table 2, heart rate and indicators of tension dropped much further, EEG (brain waves) became very coherent, and breathing essentially stopped (see figure 2.1).

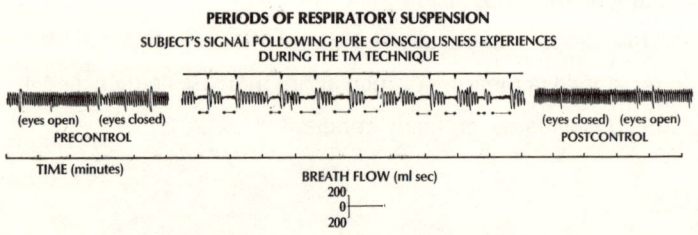

Fig. 2.1. Breath flow changes associated with experiences of pure consciousness. Subject was instructed to press a button (indicated by the black triangles) after each experience of pure consciousness. (Data from [8, 25].)

And what were they experiencing just before the button press? Farrow summarized his subjects' reports of the development of the experience as follows:

> [There is a gradual change] characterized by an increasingly quiet and orderly state of mind, by an expansion of awareness, and by a reduction of mental boundaries until, all at once, a state of "unboundedness" is reached . . . [It] is essentially the same for different people and is not affected by the circumstances preceding it, by the mood of the experiencer, or by the passage of time during the period of [experiencing pure] consciousness. The duration and clarity of the experience may vary, but apparently not the basic characteristics of the experience.[25]

Research on the Effects of the Pure Consciousness Experience on Daily Life

As for the practical benefits of the changes listed in Tables 1 and 2, research suggests these are also numerous. Table 3 is a list of the results of some of the many studies that have simply looked at the performance of TM meditators generally (all of whom presumably experience pure consciousness to some degree, at least sometimes). Typically these studies were done by comparing meditators' and nonmeditators' performances on various measures. Many of the studies were able to employ the ideal experimental design, in which researchers randomly assign people to comparable groups.* One group then learns to meditate and another might, for example, learn to close their eyes and simply rest for twenty minutes twice a day. After some time period, the researchers look for changes in the meditating group that have not occurred in the resting group.

---

*Examples of other designs: Some studies in Table 3 matched people who learned to meditate with very similar people who did not, testing both groups before and after the meditators had become meditators. A few studies simply compared people before and after learning and/or after different lengths of time after learning.

While these designs that did not employ "random assignment" are less than ideal for demonstrating causality, they at least show a clear association between meditating and the benefit listed on the table. We have argued elsewhere[84, 85] that, taking the body of research as a whole, there is sufficient evidence to support a direct causal effect and to rule out alternative explanations such as "self-selection," "placebo effects," "experimenter bias," and other problems that can arise when interpreting the meaning of an experiment. Shear and Eppley have also done a "meta-analysis" of these issues and found that none of these potential alternative explanations were supported.[86]

TABLE 3

CHANGES IN DAILY LIFE OBSERVED IN RESEARCH ON INDIVIDUALS PRACTICING THE TM® TECHNIQUE

Improved neuromuscular coordination [28]

Greater stability of the autonomic (arousal controlling) nervous system [11, 12, 29]

Faster evoked potential (brain response to perceptual events) [30, 31, 32]

Better spontaneous use of right or left hemispheres of the brain, as appropriate to the task [33]

Faster mobilization of autonomic nervous system in the face of threat [11, 12, 29]

Reduced blood pressure in hypertensive patients [34, 35, 36, 37]

Reduced cholesterol and blood pressure in high cholesterol patients [38, 39]

Increased exercise tolerance in patients with angina pectoris [40]

Improved symptoms and increased airway conductance in bronchial asthma patients [41, 42]

Reduced insomnia [43]

Slowing of physiological signs of aging [44]

Increased hearing acuity [45, 46]

Increased flexibility of perception [47]

Increased resistance to perceptual illusions [48]

Increased field independence [49]

Increased creativity [50, 51]

Increased intelligence test scores [50, 52, 53]

Improved school grades [54]

Higher levels of moral reasoning [55]

Reduced anxiety [50, 56, 57, 58, 59, 60, 61]

Decreased depression, hostility, and neuroticism [50, 53, 58, 62, 63]

Increased self-esteem, tolerance, and flexibility [50, 56, 63, 64, 65]

Increased self-actualization and internal locus of control [56, 58, 59, 62, 63, 66, 67, 68, 69, 70]

More effective rehabilitation of mental patients [71, 72], drug and alcohol abusers (reviewed in [73, 74]), and prisoners and juvenile offenders (reviewed in [75, 76]).

Increased empathy [77]

Improved quality of family life [66, 78, 79]

Increased job satisfaction and improved relationships with supervisors, employees, and co-workers [80, 81]

Table 4 is a list of the more recent, less extensive studies that have examined changes in daily life specifically associated with having the pure consciousness experience. In these studies researchers looked for periods during meditation that evidenced the physiological patterns Farrow had found to be indicators of the pure consciousness experience. Then they compared the abilities of meditators showing more occurrences of these indicators during meditation to those showing fewer. These studies suggest that the pure consciousness experience is associated with a variety of clearly beneficial mental and physical changes.

TABLE 4

FACTORS FOUND TO BE SPECIFICALLY ASSOCIATED WITH THE PURE CONSCIOUSNESS EXPERIENCE
(in Research Conducted Thus Far)

Creativity [27, 82]	Neuromuscular coordination [83]
Perceptual flexibility [82]	Concept learning [83]
Moral reasoning [82]	Grade point average in college students [82]

But perhaps another true story will be just as illustrative of the impact of the pure consciousness experience on coping with life's daily ups and downs.

Carol and her father have always been close, ever since Carol's mother died. Now, although Carol is happily married and living two states away, she comes home for a few weeks a year to renew her friendship with her father. But this year a nephew takes Carol to lunch and "happens to let slip" that several years ago Carol's father had been "doing some things she wouldn't approve of." The nephew then proceeds to supply all the details, "just to clear the air, you know — now that it's all over and done with."

On the way home Carol is mad and miserable, alternately. She thinks, "How I looked up to him. *Him*. Telling *me* to develop high moral standards. Now I suppose I'll have to go back into therapy. And what will I say to him tonight? I ought to let him have it. Really have it. The jerk. Yet I *still* love him. And he *is* my father. Yet now I can't stand him."

Fortunately, Carol has recently learned to meditate and, once at home, she decides she had better do it before her father arrives — to prepare for the confrontation. At the start her mind is churning, but after a while all is quiet. The thought comes to her once in that quietness that "maybe I don't *have* to be upset by this." And later, after she is done, other thoughts come: "It's not that big a deal, really. So what? We all make mistakes. If he were just a good friend of mine, I'd say to him, 'Too bad you got into such a mess. I hope it all ended well. Is there anything I can do to help?' " Then she asked herself, "So why don't I say exactly that?"

And that's what Carol did.

Why Those Experiencing Pure Consciousness Show These Changes: "Stress and Rest"

There is a simple and popular explanation for Carol's new perspective, for Paul and Maryanne's better life, and for all the benefits listed in Tables 3 and 4. It's what we'll call the "stress and rest" theory. It arose from the very first landmark study of the TM program by Dr. R. K. Wallace, which appeared in *Science* in 1970. Wallace's most remarkable finding was the very profound and unusual rest provided by this meditation procedure: it was physiologically much deeper than sleep, yet his subjects generally remained fully alert.

That's the "rest" side of the "stress and rest" theory. What about the "stress?" Stress is an "in" term these days. One of the most discouraging discoveries about stress has been that good changes can be almost as stressful as bad ones. Been fired? Getting a divorce? These events can create tremendous stress. But getting a raise? Getting married? Taking a vacation? These can also be heavy stressors. Which leaves us all with two choices: lead tepid, changeless lives (good luck!) or find a way to throw off the effects of stress. Which leads us back to rest.

To repair the effects of stress, we rest. The cause of stress, or the "stressor," can be either physical (getting chilled) or mental (being rejected). Likewise, the effect of stress can be either physical (a stiff neck) or mental (a feeling of anxiety). In all cases we rest or withdraw. Rest allows time for our natural repair mechanisms to do their work. If we don't go along with this basic "law," our body or our unconscious or our doctor tells us more clearly. Broken bone? Rest it. Infection? Rest. Mental trauma? Rest.

But still, some effects of stress must remain, because most people notice that when they're under stress, even if they sleep enough, they get tired more easily, get less flexible physically and mentally, get less patient or enthusiastic. When this goes on long enough, we also begin to feel "old." What we need ideally is a more efficient means of resting — one that prepares the brain for activity, rests the body deeply, doesn't require much time, is pleasant enough so we'll all do it, and above all, shows cumulative effects, so we know the effects of *past* stresses are going, not just the current ones.

The pure consciousness experience appears to fit these requirements perfectly. As Dr. Hans Selye (the "discoverer" of stress) pointed out, the physiological changes associated with the TM technique (and therefore with the pure consciousness experience) are "exactly opposite to those identified by medicine as being characteristic of the effort to meet the demands of stress."[87]

We once heard this stress-and-rest process likened to the fine tune-up of a very special car — the pure consciousness experience provides the opportunity to repair the subtle problems in our physiology, to adjust the delicate rhythms, and then to enjoy the flawless operation of a truly remarkable vehicle for enjoying life.

We can cite endless true cases about the effect of meditation and the pure consciousness experience on stress. But the following is probably our favorite.

The Feldmans decided to try the rural life "to get away from the stress of the city." They invested all their savings in an old farm. After a year of hard work, the old farmhouse was bulging with their harvest and their winter's supplies, just purchased.

Then one cold October dawn, embers escaped the old stovepipe where it passed up from the woodstove through the roof. Soon the ceiling was in flames. Then the walls.

They rushed outside. But they were helpless — even the water pump was being swallowed by flames. What good were the few buckets of water they might bring up by hand from the well by the barn? The Feldmans rescued a few things, but in their half-asleep state, what little they saved included not much of what mattered to them.

Finally Steve Feldman put a rusted teakettle on to boil over a piece of burning debris and settled down dejectedly to watch that the fire didn't spread. Ruth walked to a neighbor to call her best friend, who lived in the next state and also happened to be the one who taught the Feldmans to meditate.

The friend listened, then advised: "Meditate."

"I can't," said Ruth. "I'll just cry. I can't stand to think about it."

"Meditate."

So Ruth did, in her neighbor's spare room. Mostly it was a miserable experience. But there were a few peaceful moments when she forgot the catastrophe.

Then she came out to find the neighbor's living room filled with more neighbors, all wanting to help. Ruth graciously thanked them and said, "Actually you could get me some things from the store — toothpaste, two toothbrushes, two towels. Blue. Yes, I think I'll do my next bathroom in blue." Ruth laughed and the others took her lead.

Someone whispered, "She's amazing — so calm and brave. She's even making jokes. How does she do it?"

Ruth wondered herself.

Of course, by evening the awfulness of it all came back to Ruth and Steve. But then it was time to meditate again, and by nightfall the pair were planning their new home. And so it goes.

A year later, moved into that home, Steve and Ruth were packing apples in boxes for the winter. As they worked, they talked — harvesting their feelings too.

"Except for the financial loss, maybe the fire was a blessing in disguise. We might not have built a new house for years otherwise."

And the other added, "And this one is so much safer."

They were quiet awhile, then one of them said, "You know, I think the thing that impresses me the most is the way it seems like happiness doesn't have *that* much to do with good times or bad. In some ways we've been as happy this year as ever."

"Or happier. That's it, isn't it? It's how we take things."

"Yes — I think so. It's that some things in life are not under our control. But how we feel about them — that we have some control over."

Higher States of Consciousness

It does seem clear that the pure consciousness experience ameliorates stress. But both to those who have had the experience and to those who have researched it, this explanation for the effects of the experience is not completely satisfying. In particular, as Tables 1 through 4 indicated, the pure consciousness experience seems to create so many different kinds of changes. In fact, it seems gradually to alter one's whole style of being by adding to one's life and thought a background of silence, or wholeness, or security, or infinity — people use different words for it. This all-pervasive influence has given rise to another explanation, involving at least two "higher states of consciousness": (1) the experience of pure consciousness itself, and (2) the experience of pure consciousness *along with* one's thinking and daily activities. You are already familiar with the first, but we'll digress here a little to explain the second.

Just as the pure consciousness experience has been described in the past, this second experience of some subtle residue of the pure consciousness experience along with all other states of consciousness has been well described, especially in the Vedic literature of ancient India. But it is also in the Christian monastic tradition, among others. It first appears in modern psychology with Abraham Maslow.[88] In his study of self-actualized persons, he found that they were characterized by what he called "peak experiences," some of which sound very much like our first higher state, the experience of pure consciousness by itself. But in addition he spoke of "plateau experiences," in which people reported maintaining their peak experience along with their daily activities.

The first physiological study of this state was conducted by French neurologist Jean-Paul Banquet at the Harvard Medical School[89], who tested the sleep patterns of those reporting this experience. Compared to ordinary individuals, they were found to sleep much less, dream very little, having no "stage four" or deep sleep, and experience themselves to be physically asleep, yet "aware" through the night — not *of* anything, but just conscious.

In other studies[82] these individuals have been found to show the highest levels of EEG coherence during meditation of any subjects. And when asked about their mental experiences, they typically described thoughts as "waves or ripples of consciousness; that is, the silence would begin to vibrate and I would experience the vibration . . . as a fluctuation of . . . consciousness."[27]

In their daily life too, besides big improvements on various psychological measures of mental health, individuals showing symptoms of this higher state report experiences such as "a very solid stability and invincible strength growing in my life" and being "completely enveloped in an indescribable, soft, divine gentleness." They say, "All desires seem to be supported . . . as if doors are opening everywhere"; "I perceived beauty and goodness in every situation"; "I felt like bliss in motion"; and "there is a sense of laughter and lightness that never really escapes me."[90]

We have digressed in order to describe these "higher states" because they may be another way of understanding the comprehensive effects of pure consciousness. But maybe we need to digress in one other direction and define what we mean by this utterly familiar yet somewhat mysterious thing called "consciousness."

Nobel laureate physiologist Roger Sperry[91] defines consciousness as a "dynamic emergent property of cerebral excitation." Or put very simply, consciousness is the product of the overall functioning of the nervous system taken as a whole. Given this definition, any particular state of consciousness is the result of some particular style of the overall functioning of the nervous system. For example, one overall style produces sleep. Then the total style changes and we are dreaming. Then there's another total change and we are awake.

Clearly, the physiological changes that occur during and after the pure consciousness experience produce two additional distinct styles. These affect every part of the nervous system in ways that make us more adaptable, responsive, and intelligent than we are in any of the ordinary three states of consciousness — sleep, dreaming, or the common awake state. Thus the experience of pure consciousness by itself and the experience of it during activity are frequently referred to as two "higher" states of consciousness.

The crucial physiological differences among states of consciousness are captured best by measures of brain waves, or electroencephalography (EEG). In particular, states of consciousness — especially higher states — can be distinguished by the *coherence* of the brain's electrical activity. (By "EEG coherence" scientists mean that simultaneous measures of electrical activity from different parts of the scalp tend to produce wave patterns that are very closely parallel.[23]) In general, the more EEG coherence during meditation, the better one's performance on various kinds of tasks outside of meditation, such as being creative or solving problems flexibly.[27, 82, 83] Looking at the EEG during different states of consciousness, one sees the least coherence and intelligent activity in sleep, more in dreaming, and still more in the awake state. *But the most EEG coherence of all is seen during the pure consciousness experience.*[23]

The importance of coherence for promoting intelligent behavior really isn't very surprising, given that one's state of consciousness is determined by the style in which a multitude of parts function together. Obviously better functioning (or higher states) must mean better functioning *together*. Any manager, diplomat, general, or family member can tell you what makes for working better together: communication. And that's what must be going on when the EEG is "coherent" during meditation. All the parts of the cortex are idling together and thus creating almost identical brain waves. To do that, the parts have to be communicating fully with one another. "Dancing the same step," so to speak, like a huge Busby Berkeley Hollywood musical. (Now there was coherence!)

"Well, maybe INNER peace is possible"

As for how coherence during meditation could affect daily functioning — apparently once this tight communication among the nerve cells is established, when one goes to think a thought *after* meditation (or write a poem, try a new sport, or solve a problem) all the parts are still working together. Memory, senses, muscles, emotions — everything is coordinated. They've developed a new, better, more coordinated style of functioning. It's that simple. Thus in some ways the changes in daily life associated with the pure consciousness experience are better explained as the result of a new, more coherent state of consciousness rather than as the result of the removal of stress through rest.

Now let's consider another true story, one that illustrates well the possibilities that seem to open up when the brain is coherent.

Tricia had almost finished her novel. Several editors at a major publishing house praised the outline and first chapters — they thought it may be a bestseller. She was ready to send it off, except for the final two or three pages. They had to be just right.

And she couldn't write them. Days passed. Nothing seemed adequate on paper. She began to doubt the worth of the first four hundred pages too. And her own capacity to let herself succeed, after years of struggle.

Then one morning after meditating she said to herself, "Darn it, book. I'm sick of this. If you want to be published, just write yourself for a change." Then to her amazement she saw in her mind a typewriter banging away. By itself. And words were on the page — the perfect ending for her book.

Tricia read, remembered, and wrote it all down. She knew she wrote the words "herself." But this self of hers was far more in tune with what her novel needed than the self that had been straining to please editors or to maintain some image. The experience gave her tremendous confidence in her creativity.

As for the book, it is doing well.

Creativity has often been defined as the ability to see connections between things that most people wouldn't think have any connection. Connection. Coherence. Communication. No wonder one of the strongest findings associated with the pure consciousness experience and its growth in daily life is an increase on measures of creativity.

Artists, scientists, and business people are not the only ones who need creativity. Just living today requires creativity. As does keeping the peace, both in our private lives and in our world. Creativity, connection, coherence, communication — they are all essential. We want to be fair, we want to be lively, we want to be gentle, we want to grow — all of us together. It will take a lot of creativity.

Conclusion

In this chapter we have looked at what happens during and after regular, twice daily experiences of pure consciousness. We've looked at hard data and at personal experiences. Clearly something real and dramatic happens to people who dip into these higher states of consciousness.

We also said, in the first chapter, that something seems to happen all around these people too. But we're taking one step at a time. To start with, we wanted to demonstrate that, simply as a private and personal experience, pure consciousness has major implications for social harmony and world peace. Perhaps the four true stories have said it best. Imagine their other possible endings: Eric as a battered, resentful child; Carol and her father bitterly alienated; the Feldmans living with a lingering grief and sense of insecurity; Tricia wallowing in frustration and self-loathing. People like Eric, Maryanne, Paul, Ruth, Steve, Carol, and Tricia make up the world. They raise children, express their opinions, cast votes, and fill roles in their community. Most theories of crime and many theories of war say that all violence arises from frustrated, unhappy individuals. The world consists of a lot of individual people. They decide its fate, preserve or destroy its features, repress or support its inhabitants, and frequently create the conditions for war. Governments, agencies, armies — they are only made up of people. Germany between World Wars I and II was full of impoverished, humiliated *people*. The *final* cause of the higher crime rate in our inner cities is the higher level of individual stress and frustration.

Individual people. Single nervous systems. Stressed or rested, disordered or coherent — individuals do count. If you don't think so, we have one last true story for you.

Tony is a friend of ours, a young U. S. military officer on the front lines of the Cold War. In fact, when things in that war look hot, Tony personally controls the preparation and firing of several dozen missiles, each armed with atomic warheads.

Tony is also a meditator, and when world tensions are high, and he and his fellow officers get orders to go to their posts immediately, Tony notices a difference between himself and those around him. They get loud, nervous, and slightly more prone to make simple mistakes. Mistakes that "never really matter of course." Mistakes they quickly correct. But in contrast, Tony finds that it is just during these moments of high emergency — when no one knows if it's the real thing and everyone's *trying* to be calm and efficient — that he *is* calm, coordinated, self-controlled, and totally efficient.

"It's almost a pleasure to feel the self-mastery, the quiet inside, the stability. What everyone else is *trying* to feel, happens for me naturally. And I can tell it's that deep calm inside me that I've developed during my meditations. It influences people around me too — the other officers, even my superiors. And the men under my command are always the coolest.

"And then afterwards, somebody usually asks me, 'How do you stay so calm?' In fact, generally people are always wondering, 'Why are you happy so much? So relaxed? What's your secret?' So I tell them. Some don't really listen, but some of the guys are learning to meditate. They can see it will help them personally and also make them better at this job which matters so much to us all."

3

The Big Breakthrough: A Field Effect for Pure Consciousness

Standing back for a long look at ourselves, here on our planet, we have to be aware that we are accelerating toward something. More people are alive now than the total of all who have ever lived before. More scientific and technological advances have occurred in the last few decades than the total of all prior advances. Ecological, political, and economic changes are similarly breathtaking. Change itself seems to be taking place at an exponential rate.

The question is, of course, *where* are we headed? A prominent opinion is that we're headed for trouble, to put it mildly, because our social and emotional evolution has not kept pace with our scientific and technological evolution. Mulling over this dangerous imbalance, responsible people find themselves weighed down with a feeling of helplessness. In particular, even the brightest of our species seem stumped by the threat of nuclear war, just one of our problems.

So that is one bleak but popular view of where, with such speed, we are headed.

If you read the book or saw the movie *The Right Stuff*, you will remember the drama surrounding "Mach 1" (the speed of sound). Some thought humans were not supposed to travel that fast, that machines could not withstand the strain, that some mysterious and sinister fate awaited the pilot who broke that barrier. And when Chuck Yaeger made his flight, his plane shook and Chuck shook and we all shook with him, as he came closer and closer to the mysterious barrier. Then he was through and flying in triumphant, serene silence.

Likewise, another opinion about the accelerating changes on earth is that we are fast approaching some major transition. We are shaking, the whole planet is shaking, our rivets are screaming, ground control is begging us to cut the engines, bale out, anything! But we've got the Right Stuff, and we're going for that sublime triumph over our self-imposed limits.

Of course, to hold this opinion about the future of our species, one needs considerable faith in human intelligence and kindness — or perhaps in one's Creator! Or at least great confidence in the capability of humans to change. Still, only a small percentage of the earth's population is undergoing change through personal experiences of the effects of pure consciousness described in the last chapter.

In fact, getting down to the nuts and bolts, the DNA and RNA, the East and West, the North and South — is there any valid, substantial, reasonable basis for thinking we're going to make it as a species?

Mach 1, The Big Bang, Lasers, and Could There Be a Dawn Out There in All That Darkness?

We are all familiar with the arguments for the We-Don't-Have-The-Right-Stuff hypothesis, so let's consider the affirmative case. Let's consider whether, bad as things seem to be, we might be seeing the dawn of a radically new era.

The big breakthrough

Nature is full of such phase transitions — times when a *small* additional change creates a whole new condition. After all, in one brief moment of some little energy fluctuation, the universe began. Or consider the amazing laser: just an ordinary light source until it's transformed by a tiny but critical increase in the number of coherent photons being emitted. Or consider Mach 1: just a little more speed is all it takes. Or the tiny increment in temperature which suddenly freezes or boils a substance.

Even ages of enlightenment have been described this way by historians: when a certain number of outstanding individuals happen to appear in a culture, something in the very atmosphere seems to change and wisdom blossoms.

"The atmosphere changes." That is the key idea. Something is happening to a few of the parts, and then suddenly it is happening to the whole. When water boils or light becomes coherent, the entire pot boils, the entire light becomes a laser. Or, as physicists would say, the entire field is affected. A phase transition is a field effect. The units in the system — photons, molecules, people — all go through something at once, *as a result of* a small but critical number's going through it first.

Likewise, maybe when a critical number of people on this planet get just a little more coherent, a little less foggy — by experiencing pure consciousness — we will pass through this shaky period, "punch through the envelope," and enjoy ourselves as we never have before. It's a simple idea.

Breakthrough
The Seed Is in the Soil

As with most simple, daring ideas, all the components have always been available. In fact, as with the understanding of pure consciousness itself, the idea that the experience of pure consciousness could affect the environment has been around in a vague form in many cultures. In an example from the Christian tradition, *The Cloud of Unknowing*, written by an unknown English priest in the fourteenth century, the experience of pure consciousness is clearly described — its physiological and psychological effects, and the intellectual concept of what he called "pure contemplation." As for its social value and effect on the world, "the whole of mankind is wonderfully helped by what you [the experiencer] are doing, in ways you do not understand . . . It is more profitable to your friends, natural and spiritual, dead or alive." More than all actions or virtues, it "is the 'best part' — without it all the rest is virtually worthless."[1]

Likewise, St. John of the Cross, living in sixteenth-century Spain, wrote that doing good works is valuable until one experiences what we have called pure consciousness. Then one "should not become involved in other works and exterior exercises," because "a little of this pure love is more precious to God and the soul and more beneficial to the Church, even though it seems one is doing nothing, than all these other works put together."[2]

In the Jewish tradition, the social value of the experience called "Divine Nothingness" or "the Naught" is made clear by the founder of the Hasidic movement, the Ba'al Shem Tov. Through it "man elevates all the worlds" and "brings new life to this world, for he brings prosperity to this world (if his intention was directed there) or the world to come."[3] And Jacob Teshima writes that Rabbi Dov Baer, the Great Preacher (who died in 1772), and his student Rabbi Levi Isaac, both held that "the renewal of cosmic vitality and even the course of history is possible through man's return to the Infinite God in contracted heart, in self extinction."[4] In Dov Baer's words, "Man should keep himself in contact with the Naught so that he can bring everything together (to renew them) . . . "Whenever the people of Israel achieve the dimension of Naught, then everything gets the same dimension and our righteous Messiah will come."[4] According to Teshima, the Hasidics thought such moments were crucial because through them "God releases the exiles of all creation seeking to be redeemed, and releases the holiness of their being up to

The big breakthrough

the hand of the Creator. Not only Zaddik but also every Jew must, therefore, encourage himself to reproduce those moments of unity," the goal of which is "perpetual brightness in the whole universe."[4]

In the Zen tradition, Dogen (1200-1253), the founder of the Soto school, taught that one moment of Buddhahood brings *satori* to the whole universe, the whole world is "purified throughout their heart and body . . . every creature jumps into the same event (true enlightenment)."[4]

In all traditions there are "active" types as well — people who strive to perfect themselves and the world through "good works" (in modern terms, perhaps "social action"). While their goals are generally similar to those of the "contemplatives," there is bound to be some debate about the best means. The contemplatives are usually at a disadvantage in such a discussion, in that they appear to be merely sitting in their cells or caves or homes, their eyes closed to the problems of the world. Meanwhile the actives are busy getting things done about their problems. Yet contemplatives feel certain they affect the world around them even more.

As long as the question remained theological or ethical and was not scientifically tested, the contemplatives had no means to prove their point, much less to verify objectively what the crucial experience was and who was having it how often. (Given how vaguely the techniques are usually described, the actual experience — as opposed to the seeking and the glorification of it — may have been rather rare in most traditions.) The breakthrough on this question came when the pure consciousness experience was expressed in scientific terms, tested, and then given the scientific explanations we have come to expect.

The Seed Is Watered

Two concepts that proved central were phase transitions and field effects. They were well established throughout the natural sciences by the early 1970s. Social scientists spoke of social fields and cultural phase transitions. And physiologists had begun using these concepts to explain what might be happening in the brain during the pure consciousness experience. By now they knew that as soon as one of their experimental subjects closed his or her eyes to meditate, EEG coherence would spread among the neurons of the cerebral cortex. That is, more and more of the neurons would begin to fire at the same time until, at some point, what could be called a phase transition would occur and the whole frontal cortex would produce brain waves of similar frequency and phase relation. Also at this point the subjective experience would change, from specific thoughts (presumably arising at particular locations in the cortex) to the experience of pure consciousness — no thoughts or sensations — just awareness itself (presumably arising from the brain as a whole). That is, the physiology behind the experience of pure consciousness seemed best described as a phase transition in a field.*

At Last the Seed Sprouts

In 1974, a conference was held in Arosa, Switzerland, to discuss the scientific research on the experience of pure consciousness. It was an interdisciplinary blend of physicists, mathematicians, chemists, physiologists, educators, management specialists, and social scientists (including ourselves) — all discussing theory, research, and application. It also included Maharishi Mahesh Yogi, the developer of the TM program, who offered a Vedic perspective. In this fertile, interdisciplinary atmosphere, parallels began to be drawn between changes in the nervous system during the pure consciousness experience and various examples of phase transitions in other fields.

---

*The neuron itself also operates through such a phase transition — when a critical chemical balance is reached, an all-or-none threshold is passed and the neuron fires.

The big breakthrough

Finally, in the anthropocentric tradition of our species, someone innocently observed how a few calm, wise individuals joining an incoherent crowd can often make calmness and wisdom prevail. Likewise, the educators and management experts had noticed that a few meditators within their organizations often improved the productivity and morale of the entire group.

At this point Maharishi suggested, from his observation of changes already occurring in areas where there were many meditators, that in any group or population, even as few as one percent experiencing pure consciousness would affect the other ninety-nine percent. And in large countries, even less than one percent might be needed. He added that this effect would not necessarily be through anything meditators might say or do, but just by their experience of pure consciousness, in itself.

The room buzzed. The physicists and biologists seemed especially excited, pointing out the similarity between this and other phase transition phenomena, and how these phenomena required postulating a field effect, which then permits action-at-a-distance, and so forth. But to social scientists like ourselves, the suggestion was rather hard to digest. We went home shaking our heads.

After the conference we wrote about the idea to a sociologist friend, Garland Landrith. He saw no point in debating whether a few meditators could have broad social effects. The idea could be easily tested!

Landrith's Pioneering "1%" Studies

Using data from the TM teaching organization, Landrith[5] and psychologist Candace Borland looked for U. S. cities with one percent of their population meditating (and therefore presumably experiencing pure consciousness). And as a gross but easily accessed measure of social coherence in a city, he used yearly crime rates from the FBI.

In 1973, the most recent year for which all data where available, Landrith found that among those cities with populations of over 25,000, eleven had had one percent of their population practicing the TM technique. For comparison he selected eleven other cities, all with much fewer than one percent TM participants, that most closely resembled the "1%" cities for population, region of the country, college population, and previous crime rate trends. As expected, the change in crime rates between 1972 and 1973 for these eleven "non-1%" comparison cities followed the national trend, increasing an average of 8.3%.

But the "1%" cities followed a dramatically different pattern: every one of them showed a *decrease* in crime, averaging –8.2%! (These results are shown in Fig. 3.1) Moreover, this difference in 1972–73 crime rate changes between the "1%" and "non-1%" cities was so large that the probability of it being a coincidence — what statisticians call its "level of significance" — is less than 1 in 1,000.

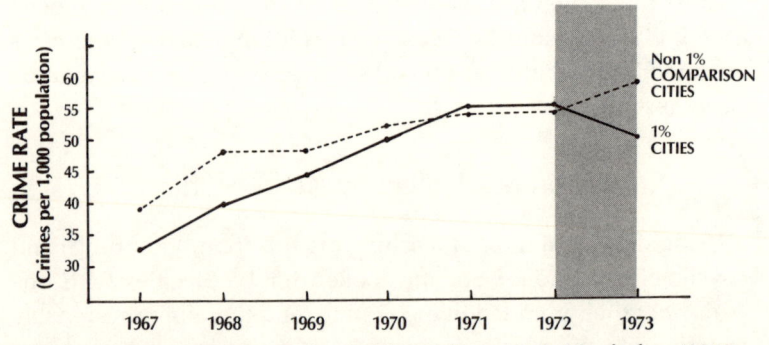

Fig. 3.1. Average crime rate for "1%" and "non-1%" cities before (1967–1972) and after (1973) the "1%" cities reached one percent TM meditators. (Based on data in [5].)

Do Increased Percentages of Individuals Experiencing Pure Consciousness *Cause* Decreased Crime Rates?

Landrith's basic findings have now been confirmed in a score of subsequent studies, some of which we will consider later in this chapter and in other chapters. These later studies have used a variety of procedures and statistical measures, so that it is now almost impossible to deny this association — or "correlation," to use the statistical term — between TM percentage and improvements in social indicators.

Often such associations are enough to convince scientists that a change in something we'll call A has caused a change in some B. For example, it is widely accepted that since, on the average, married people have better mental health, being married (A) improves mental health (B). Yet it could be argued that the mentally healthy (B) find it easier to enter and stay in marriage (A), or that some third factor (such as level of education or income) makes people both more mentally healthy and more likely to be married. But to most people it is just "common sense" that the A in this case causes the B.

However, stronger evidence is needed when someone has an idea about some A causing some B that is less a part of a culture's conception of what is likely — for example, that people experiencing pure consciousness affect others without any social contact. First an association between A and B must be firmly established. *Then* the direction of causality must be isolated — that A caused B rather than B causing A or some third factor causing both. In the present case, skeptics can argue that some third factor could have caused both TM percentages to rise and social conditions to improve. For example, if economic conditions improved in a city, there might be less crime and there also might be an increased interest in personal development such as taking meditation courses.

Social scientists can almost always think up some plausible third factor as an alternative explanation for correlational findings, especially when the correlation is highly unexpected. Ideally the interpretation of correlational results is settled by conducting a "true experiment," which controls for other possible causes. For example, in one widely used type of true experiment, a group is randomly divided into two smaller groups, one to be exposed to what is thought to be the causal influence and the other left alone, as a control group. Then measures are taken to see if one group has changed substantially more than the other. Since their only systematic difference is being exposed or not to the hypothesized causal influence, a clear change in the exposed group almost surely means causality.

Another kind of experimental design uses one group and lets it be its own control. A researcher measures how it is normally, then how it is during the experimental influence, and then how it is again without the influence. Different "experimental designs" are suitable for different situations.

However, in research with immediate practical implications, and in social research generally, such true experiments are not usually possible. In our example of marital state and mental health, researchers can not assign some to marry, some to stay single. Or an even better example is the famous conclusion by the Office of the Surgeon General that smoking is hazardous to your health. All the studies associating smoking and lung cancer were basically correlational. There had been true experiments with animals, of course. But it was neither practical nor moral to instruct one random large group of humans to smoke for several years, another large identical group not to smoke, and then to count how many in each group developed lung cancer!

Fortunately, sound research on important social issues such as health behaviors is still possible, using "statistical" rather than "true experimental" controls. In fact, no doubt because most really critical or controversial influences on humans can't be tested experimentally, statisticians have developed many ingenious ways to determine the direction of causality from correlational information. These techniques are invaluable in the study of the effect of the pure consciousness experience.

The most common approach involves two steps. First, scientists list all plausible third-factor explanations for a particular association. Then they use special statistical procedures to estimate what the relationship between the two original factors would be if the third factors were "controlled for" or "held constant" (that is, equalized). For example, a possible third factor in the smoking research might have been living in cities — the tension of city life might increase smoking and the pollution of cities might increase lung cancer. So statisticians would look only at the association of smoking and lung cancer for people living in big cities. Then, only for people in small towns. Then, rural areas. Next they would pool all these results in a specially calculated, overall figure that indicates the relation of smoking and lung cancer "controlling for" city size. This particular procedure is called "partial correlation" or "covariance analysis." Because the smoking and lung cancer relation kept holding up after all the reasonable third factors had been controlled for, eventually the Surgeon General felt scientifically confident about putting a warning on cigarette packages.

Similarly, it is obviously not feasible to select which cities will and will not have one percent of the population practicing the TM technique. Thus this "1%" or "Maharishi Effect" research took a significant step forward when psychologist Michael Dillbeck and some associates published an article in the *Journal of Crime and Justice*[6] that reported results of a study in which they had controlled statistically for the major possible "third factors" in Landrith's data on the eleven "1%" and matched "non-1%" cities — plus thirteen more "1%" cities that were smaller (populations of 10,000 to 25,000) and thirteen matched "non-1%" cities, for a total of twenty-four in each group. They controlled for every factor that criminology research has found to be associated with crime rate changes and for which statistics could be found. These included changes in police coverage, population, population density, residential mobility, per capita income, education, age distribution in the population, unemployment, and percentage of the population below poverty-level income.

Dillbeck and his colleagues found that the original results reported by Landrith were unchanged by the statistical controls. In other words, *these third factors did not cause the results*. Thus, TM-percentage increases still seemed to be the best explanation for the subsequent declines in crime rates in the cities studied. In fact, these investigators found that changes in the percentage of meditators predicted changes in crime rate better than any other factor measured!

Dillbeck also checked the long-term reliability of the original Landrith study by looking at trends several years before and after the "1%" cities reached the one percent level. As shown in Figure 3.2, the results of this analysis again supported — and even strengthened — the original conclusion.

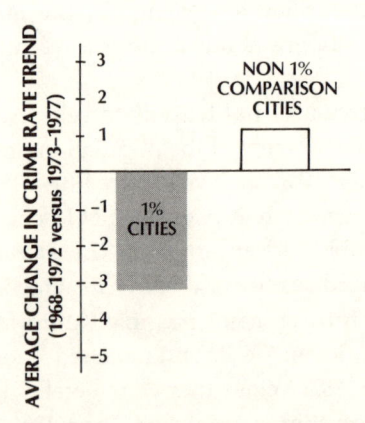

Fig. 3.2. Average change in trend of crime rates for "1%" and "non-1%" cities. (Based on data in [6].)

Then, in yet another study,[7] Landrith and Dillbeck examined the changes in the rates of auto accidents and suicides in these same twenty-four cities and their twenty-four "non-1%" twins. This study was identical to the crime study just described; it covered the same period of time, used the same procedures of controlling statistically for third factors, and examined long-term trends in the same way. The results were also the same — after the one-percent level was reached, there was a significant drop in both suicide and auto accident rates. This drop was not seen in the "non-1%" cities and could not be accounted for by third factors or previous trends. The findings are shown in figure 3.3.

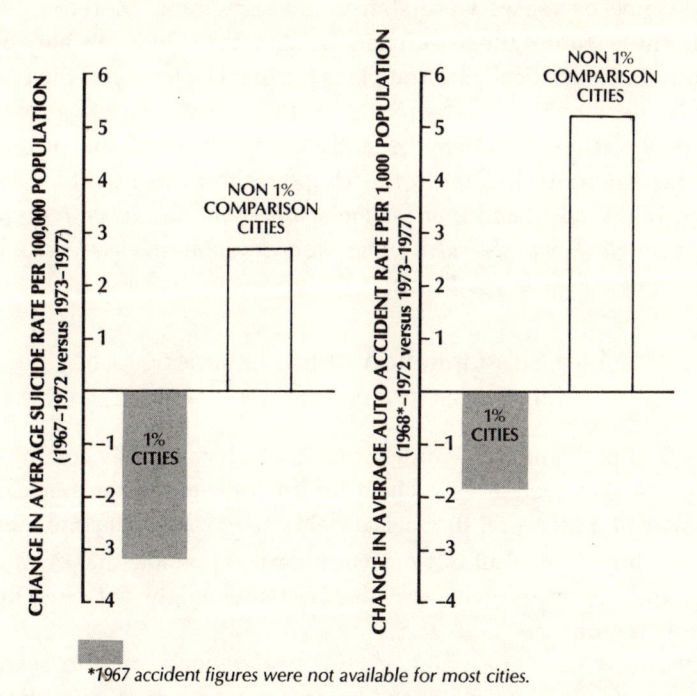

*1967 accident figures were not available for most cities.

Fig. 3.3. Average change in trend of suicide and auto accident rates for "1%" and "non-1%" cities. (Based on data from preliminary report of [7].)

More Evidence for the Basic Association

Besides working on the problem of causality, researchers sought to verify the surprising association Landrith had found, mainly by looking at other cities. In two such studies, suburbs in the same metropolitan areas with different percentages of meditators were compared for changes in crime rate trends. Guy Hatchard[8] found a clear association between these two factors among forty suburban cities in the Cleveland, Ohio, area. Dillbeck, along with Terry Bauer and Susan Vida, found the same pattern among twenty-three suburban cities in the Kansas City area[9]. In both cases, the associations between TM percentage and crime decreases were statistically significant. Moreover, in both these studies the researchers went on to look for causality by controlling statistically for the plausible third factors, and the correlation still held.

Finally, taking together the statistical results of all the studies we have described so far in this chapter, Professor David Orme-Johnson[10] calculated that *the probability of the association between TM percentage and subsequent crime rate decline being a coincidence was now less than one in five billion!*

More Substantiation of the Experience of Pure Consciousness as the *Cause*

Still, a problem with studies that control statistically for third factors is that even if researchers control for every factor they can think of and measure, the real causal factor could be the one they didn't think of or couldn't measure. Or it is possible that even if they did measure it, the available measures might not be sufficiently accurate.

Of course, at some point, such considerations begin to seem rather picky. It is *possible* that changes in potato chip consumption cause both increased smoking and lung cancer (or increased per-

The big breakthrough

centage of meditators and decreased crime), but it is very unlikely. Still, it is satisfying to be able to rule out *all* possible alternatives. And in the last decade new statistical methods have been developed that permit researchers to make an almost air-tight test for causality from correlational information.

One such technique for determining causality is called "cross-lagged panel analysis." The basic idea is that if A at time 1 caused B at time 2, then the association between A at time 1 and B at time 2 should be clearly greater than the association between B at time 1 and A at time 2. If, on the other hand, some third factor is causing both A and B, then it should affect both of them equally at times 1 and 2, so that the A1-B2 and B1-A2 associations should be about the same. (You may want to read this paragraph again!)

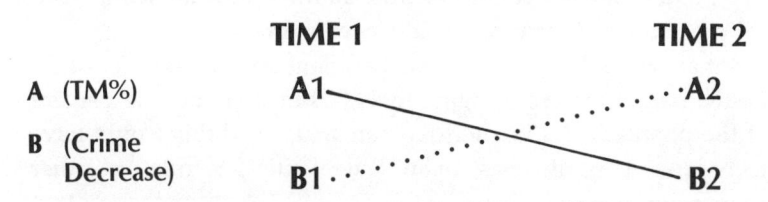

	TIME 1	TIME 2
A (TM%)	A1	A2
B (Crime Decrease)	B1	B2

Factors connected by solid line (―――) should be more closely associated than those connected by the dotted line (. . . .)

Whether you followed all this or not — the point is that in a paper presented at the 1981 American Psychological Association Convention in Los Angeles, Michael Dillbeck reported results of a major new study[11] in which he found that among 160 randomly selected U.S. cities, the pattern of associations between TM-percentage and crime rate shown in the cross-lagged panel analysis yielded unambiguous results: TM-percentage increases *cause* crime-rate decreases. Later, Dillbeck[12] confirmed the same result using a random sample of eighty U.S. metropolitan areas.

So Why the Rest of This Book, If Causality is Proven?

As we said in Chapter 1, nothing in science is "proven." It is simply accepted or not. And acceptance depends on both evidence and intuitive plausibility (given the social climate). Thus in this book we must pursue the issue of causality until it finally hollers uncle! And in the process, maybe we'll change your sense of what is intuitively plausible.

The results described in this chapter are a challenge to most people's typical way of thinking about the world. When social scientists hear about these results, their usual response is to scratch their heads and say, "Well, I can't find any flaws in the procedures, but I still can't believe it." And maybe some add ". . . and besides, I still don't trust all these newfangled statistical procedures. I want to see a true experiment."

But as we said earlier, a true experiment on, say, the city of St. Louis, would require bringing in 24,000 meditators (one percent of the population of its metropolitan area). And this would have to be done several times, or in several cities, to rule out other chance influences. (There are other possible approaches that would also be considered true experiments, but they would be even less practical for testing this "1%" effect.)

Equally important, this book has dared to offer a solution to the world's problems, not simply St. Louis', or any other mere city's. The world has a population of nearly four billion. That means it would need forty million experiencing pure consciousness to decrease global violence. Right now there may not be many more than three million. The solution might be valid scientifically, but it is not practical.

Once again, we have another breakthrough to describe — this time an additional procedure for augmenting the experience of pure consciousness, introduced in 1977. Among those using this additional technique, researchers found a remarkable increase in

The big breakthrough

EEG coherence and other indicators of the pure consciousness experience (even beyond the effect seen in the previous meditation research).

Because of these intensified physiological effects, the social scientists speculated that the numbers required to get the same social effects might decline. Thus applying the causal influence would become much simpler, and true social experiments would be possible at last. Whole states and nations — even an entire planet — might be gotten to show "the right stuff." We might "punch right on through that envelope" and find ourselves flying free in the glorious blue.

But before anyone celebrated, it was necessary to see some evidence. The first experiment employing these advanced techniques is the subject of the next chapter.

4

The Gentle Invasion of Rhode Island

On a sweet, warm summer evening in 1978 we circled a block of older homes not far from downtown Providence. We were looking for a place to park but it wasn't easy — there were no spaces anywhere near the house we were visiting. When we finally walked through the twilight to the porch steps, we were greeted by dozens of people coming and going on business, or merely enjoying the lovely June night. Not much else was happening, but we had come to see just this, a mere gathering of people that we had a hunch might someday be recalled as a major historical event.

Inside it was standing-room-only for a spaghetti dinner. Upstairs the bedding was piled to the ceiling in some rooms; in others meetings were being held. Who were all these people? They were TM instructors, gathered from all over the East Coast to spend their summer turning Rhode Island into an "Ideal Society." To us social scientists, they were part of the first "true experiment" of the social effects of the pure consciousness experience.

As we explained in the last chapter, no matter how fancy the statistics, scientists are never completely satisfied to say A "caused" B when the results are "only correlational," that is, when A happened first, and then B happened. To be sure A *caused* B, one wants to conduct a real experiment, in which B exists without A, then B is exposed to A, then A is taken away again. (Or two groups of Bs exists, half of which are randomly selected to be exposed to A and half are not).

To affect a population large enough to have major social problems, however, like a city or state or nation, thousands of people would have to be imported to have them constitute one percent of the population. The mechanics of orchestrating such an influx would be impractical and would also affect the existing population in too many ways.

So the international organization of TM teachers, anxious to demonstrate the good thing they thought they had discovered, decided to teach one percent of the existing population of a community to experience pure consciousness. True, it wouldn't be the perfect experiment because, among other things, it wouldn't be possible to ask them all to leave at some later, random time to see the effect of removing these experiencers of pure consciousness. But it would be a real experiment at last, even if rough — and the community would be permanently improved, which would be gratifying for practical, if not scientific, purposes.

Little Rhode Island was chosen because it was geographically small, densely populated, yet more politically and culturally self-contained than a city. So in June 1978 the TM teachers began arriving by the hundreds and scattering throughout the state for a summer of teaching meditation to anyone interested in improving themselves and their state, simultaneously.

Except the people of Rhode Island weren't all that interested. Many did learn to meditate that summer, but not enough to equal one percent of the population. Apparently they were too busy enjoying the nicest summer in their state's history, as you will see in a minute.

The TM teachers weren't having such a bad summer either. Rhode Island being an easy place to get around, they used their teaching center in Providence not only as their headquarters for planning strategy, but also as a place to get together with old friends and make new ones. The old house seemed to wear a smile all summer, in spite of the way it was bursting at the seams. Cars would pull up and people would spill out, then invariably others in the house would rush out to greet long-lost friends. "You came! I can't believe it. When did I last see you, two years ago?"

Naturally one of the things these TM teachers did together as much as possible was meditate. And it happened that by the summer of 1978, most of them had learned a new technique that had been available to long-term meditators since January of 1977. This new technique deserves some explaining because it made possible a crucial breakthrough in the scientific study of the effects of pure consciousness.

Patanjali — "A Stitch in Time..."

Several thousand years ago an Indian named Patanjali wrote the *Yoga Sutras*[1], which means "stitches of unity," or the verses that put together a unified consciousness, a consciousness so coherent it is able to experience pure consciousness at all times (a possibility we described in Chapter 2), consciousness that is "enlightened," "liberated," "one with God," or in the state of *"kaivalya."* There are many other terms for this state in other cultures. According to Patanjali and his equivalents in other cultures, this is the goal of meditation and of life.

The first chapter of Patanjali's *Yoga Sutras* describes subtleties of the pure consciousness experience. The second chapter details how one's life changes as this experience develops and becomes integrated with daily life. Then in the third chapter Patanjali describes a method of maintaining subtle forms of mental activity *while simultaneously experiencing pure consciousness.* This makes sense — if one is going to be "enlightened" and experience pure consciousness all the time, one will have to experience it even while thinking, speaking, walking around, and eating macaroni and cheese. But a start would be maintaining pure consciousness while having a few carefully selected thoughts, desires, or intentions. What these should be are suggested by Patanjali in Chapter 3, along with details on how to maintain them as faint impulses within pure consciousness rather than having them develop into ordinary thoughts. At the end of the chapter Patanjali emphasizes that one has these faint "intentions" not for the sake of the desire they express (for certain "sidhis" or perfections such as happiness, knowledge, extraordinary abilities), but for the sake of solidifying the experience of pure consciousness. The idea is that once the meditator is experiencing pure consciousness consistently, he or she is now ready to learn to make pure consciousness "lively" — yet also keep it as an unshakeable foundation. This allows it to become *kaivalya*, that is, to be maintained along with any thought or activity.

Once it was clear that many meditators were having solid experiences of pure consciousness, it made sense to have them try Patanjali's *yoga sutras*. So Maharishi Mahesh Yogi, who had created the original TM course, selected a set of practices from Patanjali that meditators could add to their daily meditation. In 1977 many TM teachers (and later many other meditators) took courses to learn the new practices — which came to be called the "TM-Sidhi techniques." The scientists waited eagerly for the first graduates.

According to the physiological measures, the sutras worked very well. For example, in one study[2] a group of individuals who had been meditating for several years with the TM technique took the new course and were compared to a control group of meditators systematically selected for being highly similar (and who also learned the techniques a few months later). A few months after the course, the increase in EEG or brain wave coherence of those using Patanjali's techniques was clearly much higher than that of the controls.

The subjective reports were equally impressive; many claimed that the contrast before and after learning these additional techniques, both in meditation and in their lives, was even greater than the contrast before and after learning to meditate in the first place. It was very much as Patanjali described — pure consciousness now seemed dynamic and full as well as silent and unbounded.

Because these meditators were experiencing a "riper" pure consciousness, the social scientists researching the social effects of pure consciousness were eager to see whether these meditators could affect their surroundings even more than "ordinary" meditators. Some likened it to light bulbs — on the outside bulbs could look the same, but they can come in different wattages. More watts mean more light radiated. The only problem was that as of 1978 most of the people who had learned these TM-Sidhi techniques were TM teachers and tended to spread themselves all over the country rather than reside in any one locale. Until that summer, in Rhode Island.

Providence Lives Up to Its Name

When the 350 or so TM teachers first went to Rhode Island, they expected to teach one percent of the population to meditate and as a result to change everything about Rhode Island for the better. They boldly picked a list of readily available statistics — everything from employment rate to ozone pollution levels — which they expected to affect for the better during their campaign. They went around to Rhode Island's government officials, its universities, its media — and they laid their cards on the table. "This summer will be like nothing you've ever seen. Rhode Island will be an ideal society, in exactly these ways."

On the whole, they were met with smiles and yawns. Everyone

was nice, everyone thought these meditation teachers were nice. But that was about it. Rhode Island, like every other state in the Northeast, had had its problems of crime, accidents, unemployment, pollution, and so forth for a long time. The locals figured a bunch of people closing their eyes and meditating twice a day for three months wasn't even going to rearrange these messes if the best minds in the state hadn't been able to clean them up in the course of their entire careers. And given the fact that they never got one percent of the population meditating, even the meditation teachers were having their doubts.

Here is the interesting part, however. The teachers had come to Rhode Island to conduct one experiment, but they were actually in a quite different one. While they never got one percent of Rhode Island's population experiencing pure consciousness through the TM program, their own numbers fluctuated around .04%. This was a large enough percentage to make the scientists able and eager to look for the effects of the teachers themselves practicing these new techniques, which they were doing together in groups and at the same time, mainly in and around Providence.

Walter Zimmerman, the original researcher, looked at twenty-one statistics that seemed indicative of quality of life and that were easy to obtain.[3] To make a truly accurate comparison, he compared their levels during the summer of 1978 to the levels during the five previous summers. He also looked at the percentage of change between each summer and its preceding summer for those five years. The results?

The Twenty-One Dimensions of Paradise

All but two of the measures improved, many quite markedly. Taking all the measures together, Zimmerman calculated that the overall improvement in "quality of life" was roughly 28% over the average of the five previous summers, and a 43% improvement over the immediately previous summer. (See figure 4.1) In most cases the improvement during the summer of 1978 marked the first reversal in an otherwise uninterrupted deteriorating trend. Sadly, after the group left in September, the negative trends returned.

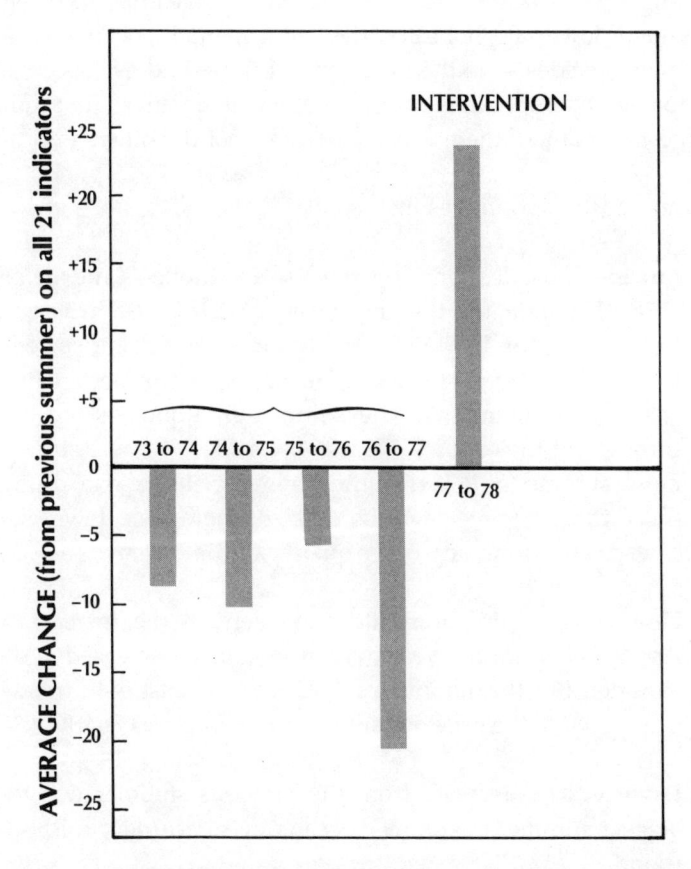

Fig. 4.1. Average change (from previous summer) on 21 statistical indicators for four summers before and for summer of Rhode Island experiment. All statistics were adjusted so that a positive change meant an improvement. (Based on data from [3].)

Perhaps the most striking point is that while in some years there were fewer murders, in other years there was higher employment, and so forth — *there had not been a single year when so many of these statistics improved together.* This suggests that none of these improvements was in itself the cause (more employment causing fewer suicides, divorces, etc.). Good weather, more employment, lower alcohol sales, the better mental health reflected by fewer suicides — in the past none of these had ever been accompanied by improvements in the others in a pattern that could suggest that any of them was the true *cause* of the others improving.

Now for the specific results:

1. **Suicide.** Suicides were on the rise in Rhode Island before 1978. The rate for the five years of 1974–1978 was 68% higher than for 1969–1973. Yearly rates were rising steadily, from 81 in 1974 to 141 in 1977. Furthermore, suicides are typically more common in the summer in Rhode Island and throughout the country. Yet there were 41.8% fewer suicides in the summer of 1978 than the summer of 1977. Also, during those three summer months of 1978, there were fewer suicides than during any other quarter of that year.

2. **Homicide.** Again, homicide had been on the increase in Rhode Island for ten years, and also usually increased in the summer. But the summer of 1978 went against both trends. Compared to the previous summer, the drop was nearly 40%.

3. **Divorce.** The decrease from the previous summer was the biggest summer-to-summer decline ever recorded in Rhode Island.

4. **Marriage.** The summer of 1978 had the highest marriage rate on record.

The gentle invasion of Rhode Island

5. **Deaths.** The death rate for the summer of 1978 was lower than the previous summer, lower than any other season of 1978, and the third lowest quarterly death rate in history.

6. **Deaths due to cirrhosis of the liver.** This is an indicator of alcoholism. The number of such deaths was the lowest quarterly figure on record.

7. **Traffic fatalities.** These began being recorded in 1975. The rate was increasing steadily each year. But the summer of 1978 was the lowest quarter on record. From previous trends, 34 people were expected to die on the Rhode Island highways that summer; in fact, only 14 did.

8. **Murder.*** During the first half of 1978 there had been a 146% increase over the first half of 1977. Yet during the time the meditators were in Rhode Island, there was a nearly 50% drop from the same period the previous year.

9. **Forcible Rape.** There was an increase in reported rapes. However, interviews with personnel at rape counseling centers indicated that they thought the incidence was actually down, but the courage of women to report rape was up that summer, so these results are difficult to interpret.

10. **Robbery.** There was a 7% increase in robbery compared to the summer of 1977. This is less than the average increase for the year or the average of incidents for the same period in the five years from 1973–1977.

---

*The "homicide" statistics described above were quarterly figures from the State Department of Vital Statistics. This "murder" measure (and the other crime figures listed below) is from the FBI Uniform Crime Index and is for only the two-month period at the heart of the intervention — a precision of analysis not possible with the homicide category because of the way Rhode Island happens to keep its records.

11. **Aggravated assault.** This decrease was the greatest percentage decrease for any summer from 1973 to 1978. It is more than twice the decrease of any other similar period. Overall, 1978 went up 5% anyway. But without the low summer incidence the increase would have been 18%.

12. **Breaking and entering.** The summer of 1978 marked the first decrease in five years. The 6% decline was not large, but the change in trend was dramatic: given the pattern from the several previous summers, 300 additional incidents that would have been expected that summer did not occur.

13. **Larceny** (shoplifting, stealing something out of a car, or other theft involving over a $200 loss). The decrease was 5% compared to the summer of 1977. The average change for the summers of 1973 through 1977 was an increase of 21%.

14. **Auto theft.** The rate was 11% less than the previous summer and lower than any of the previous five summers.

15. **Unemployment.** There was a 26% decrease compared to the same period the previous year and a 19% decrease compared to the average of the previous five summers. However, 1978 as a whole had low unemployment and the figures for the summer were only slightly better than for the year as a whole. The important point here is that during the rest of 1978 (and during previous periods of low unemployment) the other 21 statistics did not all improve simultaneously the way they did during the summer of 1978.

16. **Beer sales.** Between 1973 and 1978 there had been a steady rise in beer sales. The summer of 1978 saw the first significant decrease. (This was in spite of an unusually high number of sunny days.)

17. **Cigarette sales.** There was an increase in cigarette use for August and a decrease for July. Taking into account June and September (part-month figures were not available), the four-month period showed a decrease. As it stands, however, the results are ambiguous.

18. **Total employment.** Reports from the State of Rhode Island Employment Bulletin stated that there was a record-breaking level of total employment during the summer of 1978.

19. **Sunny days.** The summer was 14% sunnier than the thirty-year average. June was the sunniest June since 1953. July was 10% above average. August was lower than the norm — 66% rainier than the normal August. (It seems both the sunbathers and farmers had their way.) However, the increased rain in August influenced the next two factors, as rain cleaned the air during this month with typically the greatest pollution level!

20. **Carbon monoxide pollution.** Number of days when levels violated federal standards declined 63% over summer of 1977, the greatest decline on record.

21. **Ozone pollution.** The most dramatic decrease in number of violation days on record.

A Reanalysis of the Statistics

In 1983 Michael Dillbeck, Andrew Foss, and Walter Zimmerman published a "new and improved" analysis of the Rhode Island experiment.[4] They used Delaware as a control state with which to compare Rhode Island, and they employed a sophisticated statistical technique called "time series analysis."

First they reduced the measures to eight (for various good reasons — for example, they left out marriage and divorce because those decisions are usually made months in advance, and they combined the various crime categories so as not to weight crime so heavily). Next, they took the statistics month by month in the two states, for 1974 through 1980, and with the time series analysis looked for *any* type of nonrandom variation that might have occurred at any time besides the experiment. This was to see what kinds of variations are typical in these statistics and therefore not caused during the summer of 1978 by the increased number of people experiencing pure consciousness. The earlier study had assumed one such naturally occurring variation was caused by the summer season. That is why they compared summers — no point in proving there was more sunshine during the summer of 1978 than the winter of 1977! But statisticians now prefer a time series analysis because it finds all the trends and cycles and variations, even those no one would expect. (In the past a time series analysis was simply too difficult to do — it is one of those many wonders made possible with computers.)

The eight statistics these researchers used were overall crime rate (from the FBI Uniform Crime Index), motor vehicle fatality rate, motor vehicle accident rate, death rate (other than motor vehicle deaths), per capita beer consumption, per capita cigarette consumption (both from taxation figures), unemployment rate, and degree of pollution (particulates in the air). "Together these variables represent a wide range of expressions of the quality of life, including antisocial behavior, health-related behavior, health, economic well-being and environment."[4]

The various rates were summed and the resulting index was found to have shown an average improvement of ".41 standard deviations during the intervention period."[4] Overall, compared to Delaware, and taking into account all the normal trends and cycles, the change in Rhode Island that summer on these eight measures would have been expected to occur by chance fewer than one time in a hundred. This kind of low probability is what scientists call "statistical significance."

The Strengths and Weaknesses of This Experiment

As a massive social experiment, the Rhode Island project was an amazing feat. Three hundred and fifty people came and went, and their impact was measured by statistics that were completely objective yet highly indicative of the quality of life in Rhode Island that summer. The results were beyond anyone's wildest dreams — major improvements on almost every statistic. Moreover, averaged together the effect remained very clear, rather than averaging out to not much at all.

Still, the experiment had its weaknesses. (*All* studies do). This one did not — and could not — "randomly assign" comparable groups of states to have these advanced meditators within their borders for the summer. Nor could it randomly assign which months of the year to have them in Rhode Island — their summer vacations from work or college came only in summer. Thus it is always possible there was something special about Rhode Island, or about summer, or that summer, or that summer in Rhode Island, that somehow caused that time and place to be chosen for this experiment and also caused these results.

The comparison with other summers and the time series analysis almost completely rule out the influence of its simply being summer. And the comparison with nearby Delaware makes "something special about this summer," besides the presence of the 350 teachers in Rhode Island, very unlikely. Still, there is no way to know for sure. Likewise, although the odds that all these statistics simply changed together by chance are very, very slight, there is always that possibility. If you like very long shots.

At this point we usually find people are saying, "It's all very convincing. You almost have me believing this. Yet it can't be. There's no scientific explanation for something like this. It just can't be."

So now the scientific explanation. It *can* be.

5

How to Understand It All: Just Imagine a Bowling Ball . . .

. . . passing through a wall and coming out the other side without making any hole. True, that's a very improbable event, at least in the world we see. But something very similar happens all the time at the level of subatomic particles. To explain this and other equally counter-to-common-sense phenomena, physics has created quantum field theory. And while we admit the topic is a bit esoteric, one thing we want to do in this chapter is give you a very short course in quantum physics. It's fascinating stuff — we promise. But more important, you should know about it because it has put a significant crack in our "common-sense" world view, and that's the same world view that also makes it hard to understand the events and studies described in this book.

In fact, modern physics would create something more like a gaping hole in our world view if more of us were aware of its discoveries. According to one mainstream physics textbook, quantum and relativity theory have "nearly destroyed the scientific underpinnings of the materialist philosophy."[1] And for several centuries that philosophy has been the prevailing world view — that only matter is real, and all else can be fully explained in terms of matter and its motions and interactions.

In other words, while the fundamental reality of the material world is what most of us are used to, that view of reality is finished. Having uncovered a deeper level of reality, we humans are simply going to have to see the world in terms of that deeper level. And in this chapter our goal is to get to that level — to offer a logical, scientific way of understanding the findings described in this book, even if those findings seem as contrary to our usual way of looking at the world as would a bowling ball if it suddenly emerged from the nearest solid wall and rolled toward us. To find such an understanding, we'll follow the lead of the scientists studying pure consciousness effects and look toward the new world view implied by quantum physics.

A Very Short Course in Quantum Physics

Getting back to that bowling ball — the particular effect for which it is an analogy is called "quantum-mechanical tunneling." This effect is made possible because, according to quantum field theory, particles of matter are not exactly particles at all. In some physics experiments they act like particles; in others they act like waves. To resolve this paradox, physicists decided that these fundamental "wave-particles" of matter are really best described as "excitations in a field," that is, little blips of energy that spread out in all directions. These excitations are "discrete" in that only certain energies are likely, and thus they are called "quanta."*

---

*Each type of particle is actually its own field — sort of — and they all interpenetrate. But enough is enough. If you are a physicist, don't be furious — we know we are oversimplifying, but we promised a *short* course.

How to understand it all

So now you know where the term "quantum field theory" comes from.

The wavelike part of a wave-particle is very peculiar. In a way, it is only a wave of varying possibilities — the possibilities that the particle nature of the wave-particle could be observed in one or another of an infinite number of actual spots. If it isn't observed, it remains spread all over like a wave in a pond. Remember, the term "quanta" refers to discrete energy levels, not to discrete locations. (We warned you this theory would not fit with your common sense!) This wave gets around, as waves tend to do, so that some of the wave can be found outside of barriers that any self-respecting particle could never pass through. And this means that sometimes the particle itself can actually be observed out there on the wrong side of the barrier, like a spooky bowling ball dropping in for a visit.

Under ordinary conditions we can't see the effects of this or any of the phenomena that are sometimes lumped together under the term "quantum weirdness." But under certain conditions these quantum effects can be made to show themselves. One of these conditions is "supercooling" — cooling to almost absolute zero, or about –237 degrees Celsius (–459 degrees Fahrenheit).

Quantum effects are not evident in everyday experience because when you look at large numbers of particles together, and have them at the temperatures we humans live at, a great deal of "entropy" or general messing around is going on. However, when certain substances, like copper or helium, are cooled to temperatures close to absolute zero (leaving nearly no heat and therefore no entropy at all), things literally settle down. The particles in these substances start to act in ways that show their real abilities — like a classroom of kids when the principal walks in. These abilities are due to their quantum characteristics. And the tricks are pretty fancy. Besides "tunneling," there's perpetual motion, the friction-free flow of a liquid up the sides of a container, and several other "impossibilities" from the viewpoint of the older, common-experience, materialistic laws of "classical" physics.

So what exactly is this tunneling we keep mentioning? A demonstration of it was made by physicist Brain Josephson of Cambridge University, who simply passed an electric current along a "supercooled" copper wire right up to a gap — an area of electrical resistance where a current simply could not exist in terms of any form of "classical" detection — and showed that somehow it reappeared on the other side, without pushing or sneaking through the gap. So how did it get there? The current temporarily went into something called the "vacuum state" of the electromagnetic field. Josephson received a Nobel prize for this scientific sleight of hand and for producing dramatic evidence of one of the strange qualities of matter that had been predicted on the basis of quantum theory but had not yet been seen in the laboratory. (Brian Josephson also happens to be a meditator and one of those practicing the advanced techniques described in the previous chapter.)

Josephson[2] and some other physicists[3, 4, 5] think the research we have been describing in this book may be best explained and its details predicted in terms of quantum field theory. For example, they think impulses of coherence in consciousness might travel much like an electric current in a supercooled wire. That is, these impulses can jump gaps from brain to brain by traveling in a field of consciousness that is much like the vacuum state.

The purpose of this chapter is to explore these theoretical statements more deeply, by examining (a) what exactly is meant by a field of consciousness, (b) more of what physics means by a quantum field, and then (c) what the relation between these two fields might be.

What Is a Field of Consciousness?

First, What Is a "Field"?

To grasp the idea of a field, we'd like you first to imagine what a field is not like. So picture a pool table. Now imagine you have hit one ball with a cue stick. That ball moves, then it collides with one or more other balls and they move too, but *no balls move unless they are touched by other balls*. Many things operate like the pool table. They are best described by what are called the "classical laws of mechanics."

Now, imagine a number of corks floating in a pail of water. If we touch one and make it bob, waves of water travel outward and make all the others bob too.

Science has discovered that many of the most fundamental situations in nature resemble a pail of water and corks — or what is called a "field." You are familiar with a magnetic field — iron filings are moved around by invisible forces, right? You will soon see that subatomic particles are also an excellent example of a field. The solar system moves through another, the gravitational field. Organisms are said to be embedded in a type of field, and human society is sometimes described as a field too. In all these cases, when one part changes, the whole is affected almost simultaneously. That is, the effect spreads everywhere. And once the whole is in a new state, all the parts are guaranteed to have been affected at least a little. In other words, all the parts are intimately connected. Or, as Einstein put it, a field is "a totality of existing facts, which are conceived of as mutually dependent."[6]

So then, What is a "Field of Consciousness?"

In Chapter 2 we defined consciousness as the product of the overall functioning of the nervous system — a sort of whole that is produced by its parts but is also something more than those parts. Obviously consciousness can be very easily thought of as a field — each part of the nervous system affects the whole. And the whole, the overall style of functioning or state of consciousness, affects how each part functions.

If each individual's consciousness can be thought of as a field, and if social systems can be thought of as fields, then it isn't surprising that the researchers who have studied the social effects of the pure consciousness experience tend to explain their findings in terms of a "field of collective consciousness."

However, when most of us think about consciousness, we tend to think of individual consciousness. We know all individuals have it, but we tend to think of each consciousness as separate, like balls on a pool table, able to affect one another in the social field only through some kind of clear social contact (such as speaking to one another).

But from the research described in this book, it becomes clear that human consciousness acts more like a field of collective consciousness, where a bob by one cork (a change in brain functioning) means a gentle rocking for everyone. Rather than each individual consciousness being separate, the fields produced by separate nervous systems appear to be able to merge. Or more likely, the separateness of individual consciousness is a mirage — at a more fundamental level, each is an aspect of the same field of consciousness.

At the end of this chapter we will talk about some other theorists (the Swiss psychiatrist Carl Jung, in particular) who have put forward similar proposals. But our main purpose here is to examine the explanations offered by those whose research we have been citing. And their explanations are intimately related to field theories in physics, to which we will now turn.

What is a Field in Physics?

The idea of a field originated with Aristotle and has been important to science ever since, whenever "action-at-a-distance" has required explanation. When one ball strikes another on a pool

How to understand it all

table, we said that that action can be explained in terms of one ball shoving another. But when one planet affects another's orbit across the empty vacuum of space, that is action-at-a-distance and very hard to explain with classical mechanics.

So fields were said to extend out from objects — the gravitational field, the magnetic field, and so forth. But this was not really much of an explanation, because matter and energy always have to move through some sort of physical medium. (Ever seen a wave of water without the water?)

For a while an "ether" was proposed — a quality-less substance everywhere in space through which forces could travel, much as sound waves move invisibly through air. But the ether could not be detected, and Albert Einstein finally explained at least the gravitational field as being, in a sense, an illusion: objects are not really moved by forces at all — space and time simply curve. This was his famous general theory of relativity.

However, other fields or actions-at-a-distance remained to be explained. As you may remember from studying physics in school, eventually the magnetic field and electricity and light were all found to be the result of fluctuations in one electromagnetic field. That is, light and radio waves — all the waves of the "electromagnetic spectrum" — were found to be caused by the vibration of charged particles. These vibrations travel out through space as waves, and that's how they were said to affect objects at a distance.

Except, of course, this was still no explanation. Action-at-a-distance had simply been replaced by action-at-a-distance-through-a-"field." Physicists needed to decide exactly what they meant by a field, especially the completely empty field of a vacuum, across which "forces" were supposed to travel (whether as waves without a medium or particles without matter). Physics' present conclusion — the quantum field theory — works very well. Its only drawback is that it completely redefines what is "real" and "physical."

To explain how a wave-particle passes across a vacuum, physicists demonstrated that the "vacuum state," or least excited state of a field, is full of "virtual" particles. *These particles are completely nonmaterial, yet they can be shown to exist.* For example, by adding energy to the completely empty vacuum state, by exciting it, fluctuations in the field become strong enough to develop from their "virtual" to their "real," detectable state. A wave can be transmitted across a vacuum by being sort of passed along a series of virtual particles made real by the energy of the last real waveparticle. It is as though a row of people were passing a hot potato, but a person was only alive, visible, and real while holding the hot potato.

If all this seems a little complex, that's okay. The only important point is that, with quantum field theory, nonmaterial fields have become the basic realities. So much for the old meaning of "physical." All of matter and energy has been reduced to four basic force fields — gravitation, electromagnetism, and the strong and weak nuclear interactions — plus fields for each kind of particle of matter. And physics is eagerly working on a unification of these into one, grand, unified, abstract, nonmaterial field. As one quite conservative physicists put it, "There isn't anything to material reality except the transformation and organization of field quanta — this is all there is."[7] As for the vacuum state or least excited state of the field, "Everything that ever existed or can exist is already potentially there in the nothingness of space."[7] Matter and energy are no longer fundamental. An empty field is fundamental.

But so what, you say? Do quantum phenomena really have any implications for anything bigger than an atom?

They have had many technological applications. For example, they are responsible for lasers, microchips, and modern computers. But more important, many eminent physicists think the human nervous system may operate according to quantum mechanical principles. It is certainly capable of responding to a single quantum of light (a photon), and single molecules can cause the perception of certain scents. Thus a good case can be made for specific mental events being governed by quantum events. And we're about to see that the case is even stronger for the pure consciousness experience being governed by a quantum field.

The Relation Between Fields of Consciousness and of Physics

We said at the start of this chapter that many physicists familiar with the research described in this book think that it is best explained as some sort of field effect, both because of the nature of the phenomenon revealed by the research and because the production of different states of consciousness by the brain is best thought of as a field effect. The question is, what type of field are we talking about? The force field used for most communications and for most energy generally is the electromagnetic field, but the brain does not appear to produce electromagnetic waves of sufficient strength to affect all the people spread out through a city or country. And the strong, weak, and gravitational fields are even less likely candidates.

Could it be that there is some additional, entirely different type of field? An eminent Oxford-trained biologist, Rupert Sheldrake, has proposed such a field, and we will discuss it at the end of this chapter.

But there is another possibility. It is the one favored by most of those researching the social effects of the pure consciousness experience, and we think it has considerable merit. But first we need to learn more about something called the "unified field."

The Unified Field

We said earlier that four force fields have been identified, and that physics is now working to unify these four. Such a unification has been the goal of physics at least since Einstein, who devoted most of his career to the task, without success. But since his death, first the electromagnetic force and strong nuclear force were unified (on the level of both theory and experiment), and then the weak nuclear force was added. But the unification of these with gravity is proving much more difficult. Several theories exist, but they will all be difficult to prove experimentally. Most experiments to demonstrate the unification of forces have involved particle accelerators that can break down subatomic wave-particles into smaller packets of energy. But to do this for gravity would require a particle accelerator bigger than the solar system!

Nevertheless, physicists feel fairly confident about the reality of the unified field because of another successful hypothesis. According to the "big bang" theory of the creation of the universe, about twenty billion years ago the universe exploded out from a point. Evidence for this comes from matter itself, which acts as a sort of fossil report of the chain reactions that followed that first explosion. "Symmetry breaking," crystallization, and cooling since the big bang have developed the universe as we know it today. But these processes have also masked at the visible level the "heavier" quantum fields, and especially this first, fundamental, unified field. Yet all the evidence points to an extremely brief moment after the big bang when all four force fields and all the matter fields were crushed together as one and as yet nonmaterial. Neither time nor space existed, these being "illusions" requiring the as yet unseparated-out gravitational field. Matter and energy were not distinct either, or even existent in the normal sense.

Thus at the moment of the big bang, we could say only one law of nature existed — as a field that had no matter or energy but in which all particles and all existence as we know it resided in potential or virtual form. Thus this field (or something still prior to it, except we can not really talk about time extending before the big bang) in some sense caused — from within itself — the entire universe.

But the most exciting thing about the unified field is that it still exists, as the most fundamental, if elusive, of all fields. It continues to "cause" the world, spontaneously, from within itself. That is, the perfectly symmetrical internal structure of the unified field spontaneously "breaks," giving rise to the appearance of differences between the different elementary particles at normal time and distance scales. On the level of the unified field itself, however — on the finest possible time and distance scales — perfect symmetry is still the reality.

Pure Consciousness as the Unified Field

Two Fields Described in the Same (Unbelievable) Way

We have now described physical fields and a field of consciousness. Do they have anything in common?

We can think of any field as capable of being more or less "excited." When a physical field is in its least excited state, it is a vacuum, devoid of matter and energy. Yet it is full of potential or virtual matter and energy. And the ultimate example of this capacity for a field to be simple, yet full of potential, is the unified field.

Even in more excited states a field can be "coherent" or not. That is, when it vibrates, the waves traveling outward can be orderly in relation to each other or they can be chaotic (one or two ripples on a still pond, a few notes of sound in an orderly relationship, or churning water, white noise). But, again, the ultimate order is found in the unified field.

In this book we have also been describing the simplest and/or most coherent state of human consciousness — the pure consciousness experience, by itself or in combination with subtle impulses. And while the pure consciousness experience is a personal, internal experience for the individual meditator, the research suggests it is also a "collective" experience — it "settles down," "cools," makes coherent, or orders the collective consciousness in a way that is very reminiscent of the supercooling of a copper wire, for example, to let its hidden, "supernormal," quantum characteristics emerge. These characteristics are the "face" of the unified field. The social effects of meditating are the "face" of the field of pure consciousness.

By looking very deeply for these simplest, most coherent states in our internal consciousness or in our external physical worlds, we discover attributes of both worlds that we aren't used to. These unusual attributes are due to both worlds being fields, fundamentally. And we aren't used to field effects because they are ordinarily hidden by activity, entropy, or the random "noise" in the system. In the case of consciousness, normally no one would even guess it was a field. Many psychologists and philosophers have wondered if consciousness even exists at all separate from its activity (thinking, perceiving, etc.). The reality and nature of consciousness is only when individuals settle down and experience consciousness by itself. And its field effects are noticed only when enough of the field settles down, and then someone deliberately looks for events that suggest a field.

So Why Not One Field?

We have described two fundamental yet purely abstract fields — one called the unified field and one called pure consciousness. Some scientists and other scholars familiar with the research in this book have argued that what is called the pure consciousness experience is actually a direct experience by the human nervous system of the unified field. Especially vociferous are the physicists familiar with both ideas — the unified field and the pure consciousness experience (Domash[3], Hagelin[4], Sudarshan[5], Bohm[8], Capra[9]).

Others drawing these parallels are scholars of Eastern philosophy, especially of the Vedas, which describe pure consciousness in great detail, and those familiar with other traditions, such as

Christian and Jewish mysticism, and of course Buddhism, which was an early offshoot of the Vedic tradition. When these scholars (who are often practicing meditators also) hear descriptions of the unified field, they invariably see striking parallels between it and their experiences of pure consciousness and the descriptions of pure consciousness in their traditions.

Specifically, traditional descriptions of pure consciousness, personal experiences of it, and descriptions of the unified field in physics all emphasize timelessness, infinity, or the irrelevance of space and time. All three descriptions also emphasize completeness, wholeness, and unity. And they see everything springing from that unity, spontaneously and without anything from outside. All order or knowledge or "natural law" is seen to reside in this unity, in a "pure" or "seed" form.

Indeed, the most crucial similarity between the unified field and pure consciousness seems to be this all-important quality of pure order. The single quality the unified field can pass on to the diversity that arises from it is order, intelligence, or structure. This order can exist in the unified field only in some very abstract form, because for the unified field to be unified, it can't display any order or structure itself — even if it is all there internally. According to physics, it is completely uniform and nonphysical, yet it contains all the order and structure of energy and matter. A stunning paradox.

The experience of pure consciousness presents the same paradox. In its simplest form it is awareness itself, without any particular thought. Yet at every moment the experiencer of pure consciousness also has alertness and the potential for any thought. Furthermore, when the individual is experiencing pure consciousness, the brain, according to EEG measures, displays a remarkable dynamic order or coherence of activity. It is ready to act; all memory and all possible thoughts are there in the brain in potential form, but none are actually happening. Then when some slight activity, such as Patanjali's sutras during TM-Sidhi practice, is overlaid on this pure consciousness (a sort of gentle big bang in consciousness) — vibrations occur throughout this very orderly field. As in the case of the unified field, *coherence* (dynamic order) is the single quality that best describes pure consciousness. It is also the single quality common to all the diverse improvements in physiology and in daily life that are associated with the experience of pure consciousness.

What Is a Unified, Pure Consciousness Field Good For?

Given these many similarities, one can see why it is both reasonable and helpful to consider the experience of pure consciousness as an experience of the unified field. To begin with, it finally explains the diverse research results described in this book, which seem to say that wherever and whenever people experience pure consciousness, any aspect of their environment one chooses to measure will be found to have become more coherent. This incredibly broad impact is much more comprehensible if we think in terms of one field of pure order, and think of all the diverse aspects of our world — physical, mental, or social — as having in common this quality of coherence or dynamic order.

This unity also implies that if one wants to affect any or all of these diverse aspects, whether "mental" or "physical," the single method that will be applicable in all cases will be a method that increases the dynamic order or coherence in some way. Or rather, since that order is already inherent in everything, thanks to the underlying field of pure order, one merely needs somehow to bring that order out, enliven it, so to speak, by vibrating it slightly or by bringing the more active and diverse levels back in contact with the only very subtly active unified level.

At first glance, such "cures" for "disorders" would appear to be absent for the physical world, but we gave a perfect example at the start of this chapter — supercooling. When physical systems are supercooled so that their molecules are not dashing about randomly, the deeper order of the quantum level comes into play, causing tunneling, perpetual motion, and the like. Lasers are another example — ordinary, disorderly light is made to display the order inherent in its quantum field origin.

In Chapter 2 we noted research evidence that suggests that returning to a unified, subtle, effortless level of the mind — the experience of pure consciousness — serves to bring order to the individual nervous system. And this entire book presents evidence that the experience, especially in large groups, brings order to social systems. It does not change values or traditions or economic systems or governing structures but simply decreases the entropy, noise, disharmony, or sloppiness so that the order inherent in that system is free to operate.

The direction of all of science is toward unity (for example, the unification of electricity and magnetism, electromagnetism and light, waves and particles, matter and energy, time and space). The goal has always been to unify diverse phenomena under one simple set of laws describing everything. And what is the final duality that must be unified? The objective and the subjective, the observed and the observer, the fundamental physical field and the fundamental consciousness field. With the findings described in this book, perhaps that unity is very close.

To summarize, we have sought to understand the diverse and unusual research results desribed in this book by looking at another, similar scientific problem—how matter could appear to be so material and mechanical, yet on other occasions behave as if it were a nonmaterial field. And while only seeking an analogues situation, we found striking parallels between the unified field of physics and the individual and collective fields of consciousness—especially the ability of both fields to generate the quality of dynamic order, or coherence, in their parts. given the natural development of scientific explanation toward unification and simplicity, it seems reasonable to think of physics' unified field and the field of consciousness underlying the social phenomena described in this book as the same, single, unified, pure consciousness field.

Other Theories

At least two other scientific theories could be applied as explanations for the results in this book.* The first is Carl Jung's theory of the collective unconscious; the second is Rupert Sheldrake's theory of morphogenetic fields.†

Carl Jung's Theory

Like Sigmund Freud, his mentor and colleague until their break in 1913, Carl Jung always thought the deeper or unconscious mind contained knowledge that would be of inestimable use if it could be deciphered. Thus he was very interested in dreams, fantasies, and recurring symbols in artistic efforts as expressions of the unconscious.

But what came to fascinate Jung most was the way the products of his own unconscious, and those of the people who consulted with him, the products of artists in his culture, and the cultural products of other cultures and of other eras all employed the same symbols (e.g., Mother Earth, Questing Hero, Pure Virgin, Wise Old Man, Tree of Life, Rebirth from Chaos). These common symbols he came to call archetypes, and he saw these as shared through a common memory, or "collective unconscious." He felt every social group had a collective unconscious — family, community, state or province, region, nation, and species. And fundamental to all of these, he said, was the "central energy," or the

---

*We will not call the position that these results are incorrect a "theory." We do not deny the position's possible, although improbable, validity, and we have addressed it throughout this book. Only time and more research can add to that debate. But such a position is not a theory in the regular sense, as it is not an explanation of an effect, but rather an explanation of why there might be no effect to explain.

†Others have also articulated social field theories—notably Emile Durkheim and Kurt Lewin. But neither have been used to derive hypotheses resembling those tested by the studies described in this book.

How to understand it all 85

"unfathomable ground." This he described as "an omnipresent, unchanging, everywhere identical quality, or substrate, of the psyche per se," which makes it sound much like pure consciousness. Further, he called it a "transcendental, *psychophysical* background" (our italics). For example, he wrote the following:

> Sooner or later nuclear physics and the psychology of the unconscious will draw closer together as both of them, independently of one another and from opposite directions, push forward into transcendental territory.[10]
>
> If this trend should become more pronounced in the future, the hypothesis of the unity of their subject-matters would gain in probability . . . this much we do know beyond all doubt, that empirical reality has a transcendental background . . . The common background of microphysics and depth-psychology is as much physical as psychic and therefore neither, but rather a third thing, a neutral nature which can at most be grasped in hints since in essence it is transcendental . . . The transcendental psychophysical background corresponds to a "potential world" in so far as all those conditions which determine the form of empirical phenomena are inherent in it.[11]

Do these ideas sound familiar?

Jung's career as a psychotherapist spanned both world wars, and he had ample opportunity to observe Europe's collective unconscious in individuals and in national events. He felt the fundamental cause of war and violence was disharmony among parts of the collective unconscious and between it and conscious life. For example, when people deny the importance of the subjective or emotional side of themselves and insist they are always objective and logical, they will still be subjective and emotional — it's as much a part of humans as their toenails. But they will deny it and rationalize their illogical preferences and unproven intuitions. Or project their irrationality onto others — "they are dangerously superstitious; we are coolly rational." Other coexisting opposites that could get out of balance might be emphases on individual originality versus group traditions, needs for predictability versus spontaneity, or desire for achievement versus an easygoing style of life.

Jung seemed to think that if even a few brave individuals could restore balance and order and wholeness to their mental life, the entire collective unconscious might be affected. But he did not usually try to describe the exact mechanism, such as a field, by which individuals and their social groups affect one another. From the above quote, we can probably assume that, had that idea been available during his lifetime, Jung would have been quite satisfied with an explanation — and a method for keeping the peace (both psychological and social) — that involved the unified field.

Rupert Sheldrake's Theory

The other theory is quite recent and presents considerably more contrast. Sheldrake, a biologist, came to his theory of "morphogenetic fields" through the observation of the development of form in plants and animals. He is now convinced that DNA has not been demonstrated to be the primary source of biologic form and cannot in principle be that source, but only its intermediary.

Obviously this theory is revolutionary, to say the least, and it has met with considerable opposition and even hostility from "mainstream" biology. However, Sheldrake presents some very convincing research findings and makes clear what type of experimental evidence would or would not prove his theory. He is trying to do some of this research himself and encourages others to join him in possibly discovering what he calls in the title of his book, *A New Science of Life*.[12]

According to Sheldrake, a morphogenetic (meaning "form producing") field exists for every form, whether it is a species, an individual member of the species, or an organ of that individual.

How to understand it all

Or any and all ideas, behaviors, social customs, groups, spider webs, crystals, mountain ranges, or whatever. A new field develops for every new or variant form. The origin of the first form is probably inherently unknowable by scientific method, according to Sheldrake. The origin of a variation is probably random (through mutations, in the case of biological form), but it gets repeated if it is functional. These forms are not just records of what has occurred, but templates guiding the development of all forms (organs, ideas, individuals, behaviors, etc.). The fundamental randomness of individual events at the quantum level leaves an opportunity for these nonphysical morphogenetics to guide events.* Every time a field channels otherwise random events into a particular form, the field is strengthened and the likelihood increases that that form will be repeated yet again.

If we try to apply this theory to explain the results in this book, an interesting problem arises, however. What form is strengthened by meditators experiencing pure consciousness, a supposedly contentless state? According to Sheldrake's theory, to reduce crime or create world peace, some sort of thought ("I will not commit a crime") or behavior (not fighting) would have to be repeated. But since the majority of people probably already have these thoughts and behaviors, these forms should already be dominant and crime and violence should be very rare.

However, this problem can be sidestepped by Sheldrake's idea that similar forms resonate with each other. Thus peaceable people would have a greater influence on the behavior of other peaceable people. And people who have committed crimes or

---

*As we said at the start of the chapter, one of the discoveries of quantum theories seems to be that the location of a wave-particle can be anywhere and can be expressed only in terms of probabilities. In this sense the wave-particle's behavior is random, even while the field it is embedded in is orderly and predictable, because it represents the average of individual events. Einstein, in particular, felt that this randomness would eventually be disproven.

caused wars in the past would resonate more with those who are now most capable of these acts or are already considering them. Which means it should be far more effective to have criminals, diplomats, and military personnel meditating! And not a meditation that produces pure consciousness, but rather some sort of contemplation of ideas about morality and peace.

These are certainly alternative techniques that could be tested. But they are not the ones found effective in the research described in this book. Rather, in these studies, the experiencers of pure consciousness usually were not aware that their meditating was supposed to reduce crime or violence. Or when they did know the purpose of their meditating, measures of other, unintended aspects of general social incoherence (e.g., automobile accidents or household fires or suicides) were found later also to have declined. Thus it seems unlikely that these changes were the result of a specific thought form resonating with others in the locale.

On the other hand, there is a way to make Sheldrake's theory consistent with the findings we are describing. Morphogenetic fields are said to be hierarchical, that is, in layers from less to more comprehensive and abstract. Thus the form for chair is embedded in the form for furniture, and the form for furniture is contained in the form for a physical object in general. Perhaps at the peak of this pyramid there is a morphogenetic field for formness — coherence — itself. And it is with *that* field that meditators resonate and thus reduce violence, accidents, and other symptoms of disorder. (Such a field would obviously be conceptually very close to the unified pure consciousness field discussed earlier in this chapter.)

Conclusion

However, we are getting off into theoretical details beyond the scope of this book. Our main purpose here has been to offer at least one reasonably satisfying way of understanding the research on the social effects of the pure consciousness experience. Clearly this explanation took us into a world vastly different from our usual experience, a world full of quantum mechanical "weirdness" and "real, nonmaterial" fields.

But this world of nonmaterial physical fields is not really a different world. We have always lived in the midst of it; we are simply learning a little more about it. We have always lived in fields of collective consciousness too, and they are much more familiar. You have certainly noticed how different two towns can feel, or how each state, province, or country you've visited has unique qualities. We have all walked into a home and instantly felt good — and into other places that we've wanted to leave as soon as possible. And we have all seen how people who are close, especially family members, seem to know each other's thoughts and affect each other's moods in a way that is almost mysterious — except it is all so familiar. These are all examples of collective consciousness, and now you understand why they feel so real and how they can be explained.

We once described some of the research in this book to a police chief. He said, "I know all that. Every police officer knows it. Some neighborhoods have it together, some don't. And it changes, night to night. Some houses — you can feel there's trouble inside. Others are fine. You just get to know these things or you don't make it."

One doesn't "make it" either as a police officer or perhaps as a species. So if a rational, scientific explanation helps you to know these things, we hope this chapter has taken you closer to that knowledge.

But there's no rush. We've only begun to present the evidence for the case. And if theory and abstract analogies aren't your thing, that's fine. In the next chapter we go to the opposite extreme and describe the most practical and realistic test possible — the use of the pure consciousness experience to solve international crises.

6

And Still Bolder Moves: From Rhode Island to the World

For a social experiment, the state of Rhode Island was a good subject. Accurate statistics on all sorts of interesting measures of the quality of social life were available. But it was also a small, peaceful state in a relatively peaceful, comfortable country. Meanwhile a troubled world lay beyond the horizon.

So in the fall of 1978, after the success in Rhode Island, the international organization of TM teachers made an offer to "any Head of State . . . faced with a crisis which needs an immediate solution." They declared that their organization was "fully prepared, in complete privacy and confidence, to undertake measures to resolve the crisis."[1]

Almost simultaneously, United Press International carried a story — or rather a plea — from Esteli, Nicaragua, to all national and international agencies that might be able to deal with Nicaragua's civil war. It was very simple: "Anyone who can help, please help."[2]

Putting offer and plea together, within forty-eight hours, 250 advanced experiencers of pure consciousness (using the TM-Sidhi techniques described in Chapter 4) had landed in Nicaragua and the surrounding countries of Central America. In the first few days after their arrival, the violence in the area subsided and negotiations between the opposing factions moved forward. The meditators had nothing to do with local affairs and took no sides. They stayed in their hotels and experienced pure consciousness.

Delighted by these results, the TM organization decided to send more meditators to Central America and other troubled areas of the world as well, to calm down violence wherever it was occurring and to reduce stress in the world's consciousness. Thus began what has come to be called the World Peace Project, which sent waves of experiencers of pure consciousness to five world trouble-spots — Central America, Iran, the Middle East (mainly Israel), South-East Asia (Thailand), and Southern Africa (Zimbabwe, Rhodesia, and Zambia). The meditators, in turn, sent waves of coherence through the social field in these parts of the world.

The project's effects were predicted to be twofold:

1. In the trouble-spot areas, violence would decline and social change proceed without undue tumult.

2. Overall, the world would be more peaceful.

The motto was, "It's beyond politics." That is, "We take no sides. We don't care about the form of government — just that awareness be firmly connected with its deepest level. Then chaos will fade away."[3]

Of course the data on civil violence in these locales, and on the general state of world peace, are not neatly collected and published in nice booklets by the U.S. Government Printing Office. Nations in total disarray due to war or impending revolution don't tend to keep tidy records. So researchers had to rely on whatever statistics were available, on the world media, and on the reports of local observers. Thus while this experiment may have been the only way to test the usefulness of pure consciousness for bringing about international peace, the measurement of its effects could not be as exact as in those experiments that could look at orderly social statistics on crime, accidents, and the like.

But as any social scientist will tell you, there has never been a perfect social experiment. Tests are done in a controlled environment, in which measures are precise but also perhaps irrelevant, or they are done in the real world, and measures are imprecise but highly relevant. While what follows is less rigorously measured than previous studies, when taken together with them, it is also the most important we have seen so far. It is a very direct test of whether the pure consciousness experience can bring about world peace.

We will begin by discussing the results in each trouble-spot country separately — the conditions before, during, and after application of the experience of pure consciousness. The remainder of the chapter will examine the second prediction for the World Peace project by looking at press reports for the entire world during this period, roughly from mid-October to late December 1978, but especially in November, when the numbers were greatest.

Most of the results we will describe are taken from an extensive analysis conducted by Dr. David Orme-Johnson.[4, 5] Dr. Orme-Johnson received his Ph.D. from the University of Maryland and studied under students of the famous B. F. Skinner before devoting his career to researching the effects of pure consciousness. He is undoubtedly the "senior researcher" in this area. In case you like to picture our major characters, David Orme-Johnson is thin, handsome, and boyish for a man over forty. He has bright blue, twinkling eyes and sandy hair that likes to slip down on his forehead when he's concentrating.

Effects on the Individual Countries

NICARAGUA
(the focus of the Central America effort)

BEFORE

Drought, an earthquake that killed twenty thousand people, higher taxes, massive strikes, political kidnappings and assassinations, and accelerating political problems characterized the preceding six years. As of September 1978, a twenty-day-old war had killed 1,500 and several cities were partially destroyed.

DURING

October 6 to 16. First group arrives and begins meditating together in Managua. Month-long censorship of opposition press lifted, curfew extended.

October 16 and 30. Fifty-three more arrive. Rumors of attacks from both sides cease, people are out on the streets more. Life seems more normal.

October 30 to November 7. Fifty-five more arrive in response to a rumored threat of fighting. Fighting does not occur. Government begins a cleanup campaign in Managua, creating 400 jobs. Red Cross reports hospital admissions due to accidents or fighting have declined.

November 7 to 17. Thirty-one Nicaraguan meditators learn the TM-Sidhi program. No armed confrontations occur, in spite of threats and rumors.

November 18 to 28. Mediation between Somoza government and opposition looks hopeful, until November 25 when talks break down and some violence resumes. Fourteen more advanced meditators arrive and are experiencing pure consciousness to-

And still bolder moves

gether in Managua. On November 27 the talks resume and violence stops.

November 29 to December 8. Total TM-Sidhi meditators in Nicaragua number 123. President Somoza suspends martial law, plans legislation to end censorship and grant unconditonal amnesty to political prisoners and exiles. People are singing in the streets during a national holiday.

December 9 to 19. Twenty-eight of the group leave. Fighting resumes, negotiations break down.

AFTER

December 20 to 31. All nonlocal meditators leave. On the day they leave, negotiations between Somoza and the opposition worsen. Still, daily crises are few. For a while. We all know the tenor of the times in Central America today.

IRAN

Iran, with a population of thirty-three million, was by far the largest country involved in the World Peace Project. Due to problems with visas and airline strikes, the size of the group never even approached the number predicted to be necessary. (We'll discuss how this number is determined at the start of the next chapter.) But, as will be seen below, consistently, on the exact dates when there were new arrivals, violence declined.

BEFORE

Increasing opposition to the Shah was taking a more and more violent turn.

DURING

October 17. Forty advanced experiencers of pure consciousness arrive in Tehran. Four days after their arrival, the BBC notes that demonstrations in Tehran have become much more peaceful, calling the change "remarkable."

November 4. Violence increases in Tehran. Army fires on crowds.

November 5. More arrive to experience pure consciousness in Tehran. Crowds are still violent, but the army does not attack. No one is injured or killed. Then for the next two weeks there is little violence.

December 4 to 9. Still more advanced meditators arrive, in anticipation of Muharram on December 10 and 11, a holiday expected to produce huge crowds and a possible "bloodbath."

December 11. A million Iranians take part in an anti-Shah march, but there is no violence whatsoever. The crowds throw flower petals at the passing soldiers.

December 19 and 20. More advanced experiencers of pure consciousness arrive; all shooting in Tehran stops within thirty-six hours.

AFTER

All the nonlocal meditators leave in January because their visas cannot be renewed. Social disturbances increase. The Shah leaves four days after the last meditators, but violence in Iran has, of course, continued.

ZIMBABWE (RHODESIA) AND ZAMBIA

BEFORE

The possibility of any political settlement between black factions and the white minority government seemed remote. Meanwhile the rest of Central Africa was destabilizing. In particular, Zambia (governed by a black majority) served as a base for black

And still bolder moves 97

guerilla fighters in Rhodesia. The day before the arrival of the first TM-Sidhi meditators in Rhodesia, the Rhodesian government bombed Zambian guerilla bases. Four days before the arrival of another group in Zambia, Rhodesia bombed Zambia's capital, Lusaka, and anti-white sentiment ran high in the city. Zambia's economic prospects took a downturn.

DURING

November 4 to November 15. Advanced experiencers of pure consciousness keep arriving during this period. All bombings cease throughout their stay. There is a dramatic decrease in the number of deaths on all sides (fig. 6.1). Contrary to both governments' predictions, there is no large-scale fighting. An unexpected "all-party conference" is called in Rhodesia to solve its problem politically. Rural tribal people return to normal life, reopening the schools which had been closed due to guerilla activities.

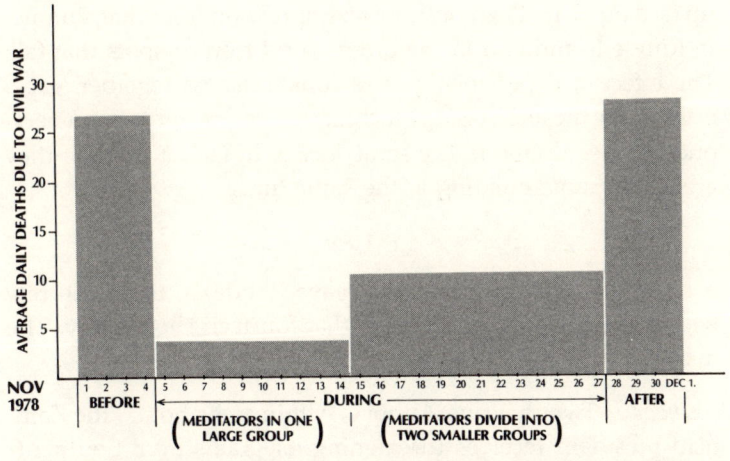

Fig. 6.1. Average daily deaths in Zimbabwe (then called Rhodesia) due to civil war before, during, and after group meditations by advanced experiencers of pure consciousness. For second part of the "during" period, the meditators split into two groups. (Based on government statistics reported in the *Rhodesian Chronicle*, as summarized in [6].)

Meanwhile, in Zambia, the newspapers, which had been strongly anti-white, begin to denounce Zambian blacks who "bully whites." The Zambian economy improves, thanks to a reopened train line through Rhodesia, a British loan, the increase in the price of copper, and the discovery of iron, cobalt, and uranium.

One Zambian government official says, "You [the World Peace Project's group of meditators] have been able to turn a very negative situation into a more positive one." Another notes, "When you first arrived, the situation here was very bad — in fact, I don't even want to talk about how bad I thought that things were going to become. But in fact, these unfortunate circumstances did not materialize, and we can only attribute this to your presence in Zambia."[5]

November 15. In Rhodesia, the group of advanced meditators divides, trying to spread their effect — twenty remain in Salisbury, twenty go to Balawago. The Rhodesian death rate goes up (see fig. 6.1). This confirms an impression from that summer in Rhode Island and in the other world trouble-spots that fall: The effect of experiencing pure consciousness together, especially with these TM-Sidhi techniques, is greater when everyone is concentrated in the same locale. In fact, it's best if they are in the same building at the same time.

AFTER

November 27. As the meditators leave Rhodesia, the death rate begins to increase. It is decided that fourteen should stay. The death rate decreases again.

December 2. Twenty leave Zambia. Within a few hours, the Zambian president receives threatening telegrams from South Africa and Rhodesia and a terrorist gang attacks Lusaka, committing many atrocities.

December 3. The twenty remaining in Zambia try meditating

And still bolder moves 99

more each day. There is no further violence, and the terrorist gang is caught.

December 5 to 22. No further warfare in Zambia. Largest turnout ever for national election in Zambia.

December 22. All the nonlocal meditators (that is, almost all) leave Zambia.

December 23. Rhodesia resumes bombing Zambia.

ISRAEL

BEFORE

In the 1970s one percent of Israel's population was practicing the TM technique. Immediately after that number was reached, and before the World Peace Project, President Anwar Sadat of Egypt made his famous peace initiative and the Camp David agreement occurred. However, at the time of the World Peace Project, the entire area continued to be unstable. (And still is, of course. While Israel may have one percent of its people meditating, the surrounding countries have very few meditators, much less these advanced meditators using the TM-Sidhi techniques. Since the World Peace Project, there have been other attempts to assemble in the area large numbers who could experience pure consciousness together. In fact, the biggest attempt so far is described in Chapter 8. But the first try was this one, during the 1978 World Peace Project.)

DURING

Because Israel already has so many meditators, instead of bringing in advanced meditators, more of the local meditators are simply taught the TM-Sidhi techniques. Non-Israelis can also attend (it appeals to many to take the course and cool down the Middle East situation simultaneously). A total of four hundred are assembled in the town of Safad. During the course, the town has a zero crime rate.

As an experiment, the World Peace Project's effort in Israel raises special issues. The attendees' experiences of pure consciousness change — gradually deepening and lengthening during the course, as they learn the new techniques. And with one percent already in the country, one would expect the main effect of the large Israel course to be on the region and on the world as a whole more than on Israel in particular. (And this may well have been the case. See next section, on global effects of the World Peace Project.)

AFTER

When the large number of new but nonlocal advanced meditators disperse to their various homelands after the course, the situation in the Middle East worsens severely, although relatively little violence occurs within the borders of Israel itself, which is still a "1%" country.

SOUTHEAST ASIA

BEFORE

Continual war.

DURING

The least data were collected in southeast Asia. However, during the presence of the World Peace Project team, Thailand and Malaysia vow to work for peace in southeast Asia. Cambodia seeks to strengthen its ties with the rest of the world. And the United States normalizes relations with China.

AFTER

One hundred fifty TM teachers (who also practiced the TM-Sidhi techniques) remain after January, hoping to implement a long-term plan to instruct and leave behind large numbers of local meditators. But the plans can not be implemented, so they leave. In 1979 Vietnam invades Cambodia and China invades Vietnam. The project organizers say, "The world should know that this war, and all other wars, could easily have been avoided."[6]

Effects on the World

It was also predicted that the concentration of individuals having deep experiences of pure consciousness in these diverse world trouble-spots would create a measurable global effect. Dr. Orme-Johnson attempted to evaluate this hypothesis as rigorously as possible. He had a group of research assistants systematically identify and count news items relevant to world peace that appeared before, during, and after the World Peace Project dates (roughly October 12 to December 31, 1978). News publications with large circulations and less local bias *(Newsweek, Time, International Herald Tribune)* were used.

In order to eliminate any possible unconscious bias which might have caused them unintentionally to find more peace-related articles during, the intervention periods, Orme-Johnson did not tell his research assistants the purpose of the research. Their instructions were to read thoroughly and locate all news items in these publications describing any of the following:

1. General statements by national leaders or high-ranking government officials expressing aspirations towards peace.

2. Policy statements expressing a motivation to progress towards peace.

3. Progress towards arms limitations or peace treaties.

4. Signs of normalization of relationships between enemies or potential enemies, such as increased communication, open-

ings of diplomatic relations, open borders, or increased trade.

5 Peaceful solutions that averted expected conflict in national and international animosities.

6. Reductions in violence.

Figure 6.2 shows the results of Orme-Johnson's analysis: a dramatic increase in "peace items" during November, when the largest number of meditators were in the various trouble-spot countries.

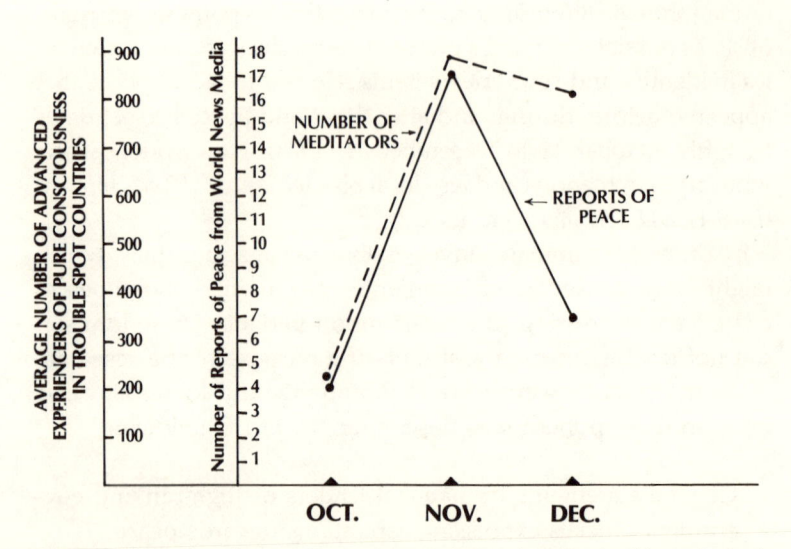

Fig. 6.2. Reports of peace in content analysis of major world media and average numbers of advanced experiencers of pure consciousness in trouble-spot countries during October, November, and December 1978. (Based on data in [6].)

A second analysis of world news, using just *Time* and *Newsweek*, compared the ten weeks during the entire project period (approximately mid-October to the end of the year) to the

And still bolder moves

preceding ten weeks (August 1 to October 12). In this analysis, Orme-Johnson reports that the number of peace items more than doubled during the project.*

More vivid than graphs and figures is a reading of some of the events they represent. The following list shows that clearly something significant was happening during these months.

Summary of International Press
Reports of Peace During the Project

October 13. Continued optimism for Egyptian-Israeli peace negotiations. (*Newsweek*)

October 16. Rhodesian white-minority leader Smith decides to allow the United States another opportunity to meet with him "and urge him to sit down with the guerrilla forces." (*Newsweek*)

October 20. Zaire-Angolan relations improve. (*Weekly Review*)

October 22. Kenya's new president is installed without violence. "All the prophets of doom have been proved wrong. I am confident we can contain any situation if we are seriously concerned with peace and stability." (*Time*)

October 25. President Castro declares increasing friendship toward Cuban exiles in the United States, "something that was unthinkable only a couple of months ago." (*International Herald Tribune*)

---

*Was it just a peaceful time of year? An analysis of other autumns might have been useful, but perhaps just the unpeaceful mood of the world during the same period in 1983 (the U.S. military action in Grenada, the bombings and fighting in Lebanon, the deployment of Euromissiles, the Soviets walking out of the disarmament talks) is enough to convince us that this is not always a peaceful time of year!

October 25. Soviet President Brezhnev strongly emphasizes to U.S. Secretary of State Vance that the superpowers should work closely together to solve international problems. (*International Herald Tribune,* November 17)

November 5. Commander of Combined Operations in Rhodesia declares, "We have turned the corner away from a rather serious outlook." (*The Sunday Mail*)

November 6. Japan and China ratify a Treaty of Peace and Friendship. (*Time*)

November 7. Cambodian foreign minister reestablishes ties with noncommunist Southeast Asian countries. (*Newsweek*)

November 7. "The Soviet Union, on the threshold of a new phase of relations with the United States, is seeking active superpower collaboration to manage international problems and head off potential clashes . . . Mr. Brezhnev said . . . the world's two most powerful nations must find ways to work together more closely." (*International Herald Tribune*)

November 10. Chinese Deputy Premier Deng says there is no likelihood of North Korea starting war. (*Far Eastern Economic Review*)

November 10. Thailand Prime Minister declares intention to be on good terms with all nations and to keep peace in that part of the world. "Any action that does not support the principle of peace, I do not like." (*Far Eastern Economic Review*)

November 10. Argentina and Chile peacefully negotiate sea rights near Cape Horn. (*International Herald Tribune*)

November 10. Cambodia allows U.S. journalists to visit country. (*International Herald Tribune*)

November 11. Speaking for the Southeast Asian nations, Malaysian Prime Minister declares them to be a zone of peace, free-

And still bolder moves

dom and neutrality — to be kept free of interference, subversion or incitement. (*New Straits Times*)

November 18. President Carter says, "I think in recent weeks there has been an alleviation of tension between us [U.S.S.R. and U.S.] and I would like to see it continue. I can't say why there has been an improvement in U.S.-Soviet relations." (*International Herald Tribune*)

November 22. Cuban Foreign Minister says his country's troops would withdraw from Africa if asked to go. (*Daily Nation*)

November 25. Leaders of Warsaw Treaty Organization propose that the five nuclear powers have talks on banning nuclear weapons. (*Radio Moscow*)

November 25. India's External Affairs Minister expresses India's efforts towards peace: "We seek friendship with all, we bear ill-will towards none." (*Hindustan Times*)

November 27. President Castro promises release of three thousand political prisoners. (*International Herald Tribune*)

November 27. Black Rhodesian leader says to a crowd of five thousand, "I have come to talk about peace. I have come on a sacred mission to stop the unnecessary death of our children." (*The Herald*)

November 29. King Juan Carlos of Spain says terrorism can be dealt with by peaceful means. (*International Herald Tribune*)

November 29. Soviet President Brezhnev emphasizes to U.S. Senators the importance of world peace and the removal of the nuclear threat. (*Des Moines Register headline*)

November 30. "No nation is openly engaged in open warfare at the moment — A historic rarity." (*Des Moines Register*)

December 1. President Somoza agrees to a plebiscite in Nicaragua. (*International Herald Tribune*)

December 1. Treaty of friendship between Soviet Union and Vietnam. (Radio Moscow)

December 7. Averill Harriman says of Soviet President Brezhnev, "There is no man in the world who has a greater desire to do all that he can to prevent nuclear war." (*International Herald Tribune*)

December 9. "The fighting [between Tanzania and Uganda] is virtually over." (BBC)

December 9. Namibian elections proceed without expected violence. "The elections appeared to be a turning point for Southwest Africa." (*International Herald Tribune*)

December 26. President Carter says, "We've got peace on earth right now and we hope to keep it that way." (*International Herald Tribune*)

The Strength of These Results

Of course, there were similar news items before and after this period — but as we saw in the quantitative analysis, there were far fewer. And, of course, many of these items could be dismissed as mere talk or propaganda. But in international affairs, talk sets the tone of events, and there appears to have been an unusual amount of peaceful talk — as well as events — during the World Peace Project.

After doing this analysis in 1979, Orme-Johnson learned that the same type of data had been gathered independently by the University of North Carolina's Conflict and Peace Data Bank (COPDAB).[7] Its figures are based on expert ratings of international news events on a fifteen-point conflict-cooperation scale. The data bank has been gathering data for some years. It is internationally respected and widely used among peace and conflict researchers. COPDAB is completely independent of the World Peace Project or any of the researchers or others connected with

And still bolder moves 107

it. An analysis of the before, during, and after periods of the World Peace Project using the COPDAB data yielded the same conclusions as the original analysis: there was much less international conflict during the World Peace Project.

Conclusions from the World Peace Project

Both quantitative and qualitative analyses of the World Peace Project suggest the following conclusions:

1. When the groups arrived and began experiencing pure consciousness in the trouble-spot countries, there was an immediate reduction in violence in those countries.

2. While they were present, life became more normal and there was progress toward peaceful solutions to problems.

3. When the groups divided into smaller groups or their numbers were augmented, predictable changes occurred.

4. When they left, violence increased.

5. The world as a whole enjoyed a period of unusual peace.

Yet another conclusion might be that the project should never have stopped, except that this rushing around to put out fires is no way to run a world. The World Peace Project was undoubtedly an expensive campaign for a nonprofit organization. Nor could the individuals in these groups be expected to remain indefinitely in foreign locales. Most were citizens of the United States, Canada, and the western European countries, with lives of their own to lead and incomes to earn. The project was only a demonstration to governments and their citizens of what could be done, and sadly, of what would happen when it was not continued.

It seems that we humans are often slow to adjust to the possibility that our troubles can be solved, especially when the troubles are so old and the solution sounds so simple. After each study it has seemed to those involved that here, at last, was enough evidence to satisfy anyone. Not only was the pure consciousness experience associated with reductions in crime, but it appeared to *cause* this reduction and create an improvement on all available statistical measures of the quality of social life, not only in cities, but in states and countries. The improvement was not only in social statistics but in world peace itself.

Still, the world remained incredulous in 1979. Meanwhile, still more evidence came in to make that incredulity itself more and more incredible. A whole new series of studies were performed, on a variety of states and nations, using the old measure of crime plus all kinds of new ones. In the next chapter we will discuss three of these.

7

Still More Evidence

It is time to introduce you to some of the people who travel far from their homes to try to bring some peace and progress through their naturally occurring but highly developed ability to experience pure consciousness. It is good to remember they are not mere numbers in an equation. They are not saints either. Or "yogis." Or anything strange or unfamiliar to us. They are simply people like you and me.

For example, Chuck is an auto mechanic in Atlanta. Dan is a pediatrician in Pennsylvania. Dan's wife, Kate, has a teenage son by a previous marriage and two new babies. Sarah is a nurse. Her husband, Mike, sells displays to grocery stores. Frank does quality control for a major food processor. Karen is an accountant for a satellite-TV-dish firm, although she'd like to go back to graduate school and finish her Ph.D. in speech and communication. Lynn does technical writing in the Silicon Valley. Josh does psychotherapy in Toronto. Clay is a philosophy professor in Virginia. The Wallisons play in a major symphony orchestra. George plays on the local softball team when he's done painting houses for the day. And so the list goes — at least twenty thousand of them in North America alone, and many more than that in the rest of the world.

In this chapter we will talk about an equation and then describe some interesting experiments. But it is good to keep in mind that all this "hard data" was made possible because of real people. Some of them had never been out of their own countries until they chose to meet with others in distant places in order to be together and affect the world. They used up vacations and savings, but then they also had fun, bought interesting things, took photos, and got in a little sightseeing. They were extraordinary in their effects, but not in the details of their lives. They simply wanted to do what they could for the world and knew that in this case they were the only ones who could do it. So they made these journeys.

Some Important Questions, Like "How Many Does it Take?" And Some Answers

Now that you know these advanced meditators as people, let's get back to thinking about them as numbers. You are probably asking the same questions the scientists were asking after the Word Peace Project: Why does it seem to help to have people experience pure consciousness in a group, in one locale, at the same time? How big a group does it take to affect a given population?

The scientists had already noticed that these advanced meditators preferred to experience pure consciousness together in groups. The meditators coming to Rhode Island, their hanging around Providence, their traveling together to Iran and Nicaragua and Thailand, and so forth, wasn't just for altruistic reasons.

Still more evidence

They felt their experiences were greatly enhanced when they meditated in groups.

People didn't suddenly discover this when they started using the TM-Sidhi techniques. Meditators have preferred "group meditations" for probably as long as meditation has been practiced. In fact, people have been gathering together to intensify their inner experiences since the dawn of history.

But why do these advanced experiencers of pure consciousness have more potent effects on themselves and their social field when they meet together? Perhaps it is like an individual neuron versus one acting within a larger nervous system. The individual neuron can respond to stimuli, but that's about it. On the other hand, when it is a part of a nervous system, it can think, move the body, and comprehend and influence the environment. In a social field, we said the one affects the whole, the whole affects the one. But the effect of the whole on the one is usually going to be greater. However, there are levels of organization between the lone individual and the whole population. When a few act together, then the few can affect the whole and usually do. A few cells govern the beating of the whole heart, a few animals direct the entire herd. How many individuals acting together affect a social situation? That depends on just how "together" they are. And that leads us to our next question.

In Chapter 4 we said that the scientists thought those using the TM-Sidhi techniques, with their much greater brain wave coherence and clearer experiences of pure consciousness, might differ from other meditators the way a strong light bulb differs from a weak one in wattage. Actually, however, when the scientists saw the effects of these people in Iran and Nicaragua and Rhodesia, they began to think they were more like lasers than light bulbs!

A laser is different from the strongest ordinary light bulb in that a laser's photons (or wave-particles of light) have been made coherent. The measure of the intensity of light generated by coherent photons — laser light — is figured to be the *square* of the number of these photons. This is called "superradiance."

Meanwhile, back in the world of ordinary light bulbs, the intensity of light produced by incoherent photons is merely measured by adding their numbers. Therefore, to equal the light put out by eight coherent photons, one needs sixty-four incoherent ones. Or to put it differently, theoretically you only need to add eight coherent photons to fifty-six incoherent ones to turn them all into a laser and get all the photons acting coherently (a process called "stimulated emission"). The effect of coherence gets more impressive as you go up in number — nine to affect eighty-one, ten to affect one hundred — or how about a thousand to affect a million!

However, the research suggests that meditators even without the TM-Sidhi techniques are already having a dramatic effect on the social field compared to persons not experiencing pure consciousness. So that also has to be taken into account. The following formula has proven most fruitful. To have an effect on a population of a given size, the number of advanced meditators required would be roughly the square root of one percent of the population to be affected. The one percent refers to the fact they are already meditating; the square root, to their "advanced" abilities.

An example will help. To affect nine million (a large state or small country), one would need ninety thousand "ordinary" experiencers of pure consciousness (one percent). But following the laser analogy, one would only need the square root of one percent, or three hundred, if these same people were, in addition, doing the TM-Sidhi program together in a group.

This effect has been given a variety of names — the "superradiance effect," the "group dynamics of consciousness," and, in honor of the person whose teaching has made it a practical reality, it is also called the "Maharishi Effect." The latest name is

Still more evidence 113

"Maharishi's Technology of the Unified Field" — a name giving credit to both who and what make it possible.

Three Experiments

The rest of this chapter describes experiments conducted in Holland, Puerto Rico, and the territory of Delhi in India. In all cases the "intervention" was an assemblage of persons who meditated together and also used the techniques described in Chapter 4 to "enliven" and stabilize their experience of pure consciousness. The locales for these gatherings were not chosen because of crises in their vicinity. Rather, they happened to be the locations of convenient places to meet. Because these "advanced meditators" find their meditations are more profound and the effects more lasting when they meditate together, they are highly motivated to meet. But they still want the location to be as close and inexpensive as possible, or to have some extra virtue to make it attractive.

This is not to say that people came to the gatherings in Holland, Puerto Rico, and Delhi entirely for personal reasons. They called their meetings "World Peace Assemblies," and these assemblies were scattered around the globe not only to spread the burden of travel among the world's TM-Sidhi meditators, but also to spread their effect and to bring it to any areas especially in need of a little more coherence.

But these meetings were not intended to be experiments in the same sense as the World Peace Project. The primary purpose was to gather together and the secondary purpose was to gather data. By the early eighties, when these three studies were done, things were happening too fast for consultation with the social scientists before every large meeting. These people were confident it was good for them and the world to get together, and they did so as often as possible.

Of course the social scientists could not resist looking at the effects of the gatherings after they had occurred. The problem was how to demonstrate without a doubt that any changes that occurred during the meetings were caused only by the meetings themselves. The scientists had not been able to choose the dates randomly — the meetings were usually during Christmas or winter vacations, or the summer season with its potential for vacations. This raised the obvious question of whether the changes were merely due to the time of year.

Fortunately, by the eighties a new statistical method had been developed to answer questions of this kind. It is called a "time series analysis." We've briefly described in Chapter 4, because the Rhode Island statistics were reanalyzed with this method. But it deserves more comment now because this statistical technique was used in two of the three studies reported in this chapter — Puerto Rico and Delhi — and in most of the studies described in the rest of the book.

A time series analysis requires first gathering a long series of daily, weekly, or monthly measures of something such as crime. Besides taking data for the time when the intervention occurred, the researchers also take many "data points" for a long time before and after. Then they tally up all the variations for the intervention and nonintervention periods — "two more on this day, four more the day after, six less the day after that, two more the day after that," and so forth. Next, these variations are all put into a sort of pie (actually, into a computer), and the time series analysis cuts out the piece of that "change pie" that is purely random or "noise" — that is, the part of the changes that shows no trend or consistent pattern during all the months or years being analyzed. It also cuts out the part of the change that does show trends — all that would be expected from ongoing trends or consistent cyclical patterns that were typical of the time period being studied. These might be changes on weekends or during certain seasons or a general trend of increase or decrease across the whole time period.

Then the question is, when you look only at the time periods when the "intervention" was taking place, is there any pie left? If there is, that piece of the change pie has to be due to something other than random or normal cycles or variations. And that something else, presumably, is the intervention.

Of course, some event besides the large gathering could be the real cause of the unexplained change. But it would have to be an unusual event — not one that has happened repeatedly in the area — or it would already have come out with the pie slice for general trends or patterns. So you simply look for any other event at the time of the intervention that might affect crime, or whatever statistic one is considering.

Obviously, if one feels certain that these experiencers of pure consciousness could not be having any effect, one can argue that all sorts of subtle, unrecorded events could have been happening at the time and caused the change. But one has to consider the many campaigns and enormous expenditures of time and energy that have been applied in the effort to decrease crime and violence, to continue that example, and the results are generally very meager. To say a major decline could be caused by "most anything" defies the facts. Remember how Chapter 4 described Rhode Island's recent past? It is sad to say, but especially from 1972 to 1982, improvements in measures of the quality of life, such as crime, were very rare.

Now, on to the specific studies. We'll take them in the order they occurred.

Holland

According to the square-root-of-1% formula, it would take about 376 advanced experiencers of pure consciousness meditating together to affect Holland. This was achieved twice prior to May 1982 when this study was done. The first time was August 1 to 15, 1981, and the second time was December 19, 1981 to January 3, 1982. Also, from December 22, 1978 to January 20, 1979 there was a gathering of 950 in Germany which, according to the formula, was enough to affect Holland (as well as Germany and Denmark). Therefore these three periods were studied by the team of scientists from Rotterdam.[1]

The statistics used were crime and auto accident rates, both obtained from the Dutch government. A time series analysis was not possible because not enough statistics for nonintervention months were available at the time of the study. However, an alternate procedure was employed that accomplishes much the same thing. First, the expected crime rate for each of these months — August, December, and January — was computed by averaging the months before and after. This was done both for the year in which the intervention occurred and also for each of the preceding ten years. Next, the actual crime rates were subtracted from expected crime rates, giving a figure that was "actual crimes versus expected crimes" for each year. Finally, the actual versus expected figures for the intervention period were compared to those for the same month in the previous ten years. The same analysis was conducted for auto accidents.

The results for the three different months are shown in figure 7.1. The base line is the month's expected crime or accident rate for any given year, so what is plotted is the variation from that for each year. You can see that for the year of each of the three gatherings, the decrease was much greater. The formal statistical analysis showed that in all three months crime rate dropped "significantly" (that statistical term meaning too much to be expected by chance) compared to what would be expected from changes in the same months in previous years. The decline in traffic accidents was statistically significant only for January 1979.

Still more evidence

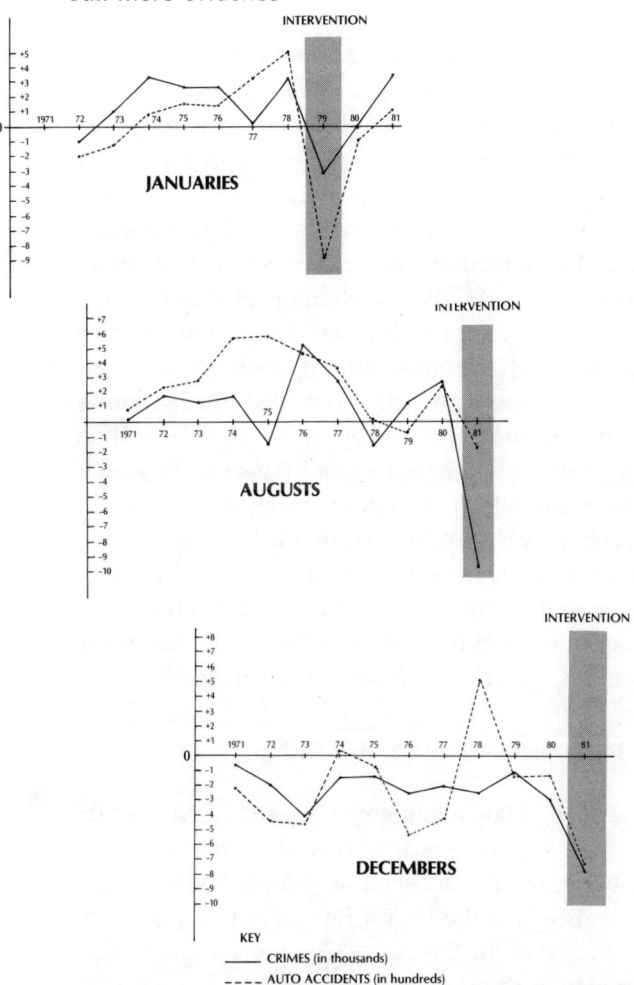

Fig. 7.1. One month increases or decreases (compared to expected levels) of crime and auto accidents in Holland over several years for months in which, during one of the years, the number of advanced experiencers of pure consciousness meditating together was sufficient to exceed the critical number predicted to affect the entire country. The times when the critical number was exceeded were January 1979, August 1981, and December 1981. (Based on data in preliminary report of [1].)

An important point (we'll be making it often) is that in the 129 months studied during which enough advanced experiencers were not meditating together in one place, there was only one month in which Holland's crime and traffic accident rates both showed substantial drops. In contrast, in all three of the intervention months, both crime and traffic accidents did drop together. Thus it does seem that something was causing both to change, and that "something" was the three gatherings of meditators.

A hindrance to what would probably have been even stronger results was the fact that the government statistics were all monthly, and none of these gatherings coincided exactly with a calendar month. In fact, none of the meetings covered more than two-thirds of any month. Therefore the month used in the analysis was simply the one in which most of the meeting occurred. In two cases the meeting was also held during a few days of the month before (December for the January 1979 course) or after (January for the December 1981 course), making the comparison of the meeting month to month before and after much less likely to show an effect. But the effect was seen, nevertheless.

The Territory of Delhi, India

In November of 1980, 3,000 meditators gathered in New Delhi to experience pure consciousness together. Over the following months the number gradually declined, as people had to return home. The area studied was the Union Territory of Delhi, which has a role similar to that of the District of Columbia in the United States, and a population then of about six million.

The number predicted to be needed to affect the state was 245 — the square root of one percent of the population. However, it was not known whether larger numbers, like 3,000, would affect a small area more intensely or simply spread over a larger area. (The latter has seemed to be the case.) Therefore the intervention in Delhi was considered to last as long as at least 245 were

Still more evidence

present, which was until April 1981. If more were present, they were assumed to be affecting the states around Delhi.

Reenter Michael Dillbeck. Michael earned his doctorate in psychology at Purdue University. He is in his thirties, of medium height, with light brown hair and a sweet smile. He is a quiet kind of guy. Yet there is something exceptional about his unobtrusiveness — he's invariably sensitive to others and intelligent-bordering-on-wise. Everybody, absolutely everybody, seems to like Michael Dillbeck.

Michael, with Ken Cavanaugh from the University of Washington and the Dutch psychologist, William van den Berg, calculated daily crime rates per thousand for every day between June 1980 and March 1981 — the latest statistics available at the time of the study.[2] These daily figures were used to find the patterns — or lack of patterns — in Delhi's crime rate. Returning to our analogy, we can call this removing the first several slices of the pie.

Delhi's typical crime patterns found by these researchers explained very well the changes in crime rate before the intervention. No pie left in the pan. But during the time that 245 advanced meditators were in Delhi, there was a dramatic change in the crime rate — an average of 14.65 fewer crimes per day, or an 11% reduction. The statistical pie slices that had emptied the pan before the intervention were too small now — they left a lot behind and unexplained. Only by adding the slice representing the intervention could the pan be emptied and all the changes be accounted for.

Puerto Rico

In 1981 a pleasant seaside resort in Fajardo, Puerto Rico (about seventy miles east of central San Juan) was acquired for the purpose of housing gatherings of meditators from Latin America and the eastern United States. The first group arrived in late December.

Puerto Rico has a population of about three million. Thus, according to the square-root-of-1% formula, 174 advanced experiencers of pure consciousness would be required to affect the entire island. Up until September 1984, when the study described here was done, the group meeting at Fajardo reached this number only during the month of April 1984. In all other months the numbers rarely exceeded 100.

To do a time series analysis, the researchers[3] obtained monthly totals for all "Type 1" crimes (homicide, rape, robbery, assault, burglary, larceny, and auto theft) from the Puerto Rico Police Department for January 1969 to September 1984. The non-intervention period was all of the months except April 1984. Again, as predicted, there was a clear reduction in crime in Puerto Rico during that April (the intervention period), a reduction which the time series analysis showed to be statistically significant, independent of any trends or cyclical patterns.

Conclusion

That's it — three more studies suggesting that at least crime can be affected by groups of people who have exceptionally profound experiences of pure consciousness together. The numbers required are not exceptional; only the experience is. People have come together in the past merely to hope for less violence, to talk about it. Why not have them come together to *do* something that works?

But you still may not be convinced. So in the next chapter we will bring out another couple of doubt-slayers. We'll describe two studies in which numbers in the groups went up and down, over and over, during a long period. And measures of the quality of life fluctuated with them, as predictably as rain and wildflowers.

8

If the Question of Causality Still Lingers

Skip and Vicki Alexander took a lot of taxicabs while they were gathering the data during the intervention in Israel. These two are both on the small side, with almost black hair, sparkling brown eyes, full and rosy cheeks, an about-to-laugh expression, and a general air about them of innocence and playfulness — not what you would expect of a Ph.D. from Harvard and a Boston tax lawyer. Maybe it was their personalities that made taxi drivers confide in them so openly. Whatever it was, after years of learning to do complicated statistical analyses, Skip came home from his first major research study fairly certain that taxi drivers are as accurate a source of information as government offices.

On those days when the number of people experiencing pure consciousness as a group in Jerusalem was above the critical number to affect Israel, Skip and Vicki would find their cab drivers were invariably optimistic and bubbly. On those days when the number was down for some reason, the cab drivers were all gloom and doom. Israel was going to be overrun, the economy was headed for a tailspin and, no, there was no chance at all they could get to the airport on time.

Later, the formal analysis of the government's statistics also showed fluctuations coinciding with the number of meditators meeting together. But it is easy to get lost in statistics and forget that when a large group of people come together to have deep experiences of pure consciousness, it is the whole social field that is getting more coherent. It is not only crime that goes down, but bad feelings. It is not only the stock market that goes up, but optimism and happiness and friendliness and all the rest.

Now let's look at two studies that demonstrate the Maharishi Effect almost incontrovertibly. In these studies the number of advanced experiencers in the locales rose and fell, and the measures of the quality of life rose and fell with those numbers, as consistently as any scientist discovering a new law of nature could hope for.

Israel

Because of the increasing troubles in the Middle East in 1983, Jews in Israel and elsewhere decided to apply the experience of pure consciousness to the area's problems (but to concentrate on Israel because it was the country to which they had access). Unlike the research described in the last chapter, this study[1] was planned ahead of time to be an experiment — and a demonstration to other governments, and hopefully a catalyst for peace.

According to the formula, two hundred meditators were needed to affect the population of Israel. Given that Israel had extended itself northward with an invasion of Lebanon by that summer, the gathering was intended to affect that situation too. But it was also intended to strengthen the country itself in every way, so that it might be more coherent in all its actions, inside and outside of its borders. Finally, it was hoped that a clear demon-

If the question of causality still lingers

stration in Israel would tempt other countries to add this powerful defensive weapon to their arsenals.

Approximately sixty-five advanced experiencers of pure consciousness were meditating together daily in Jerusalem as of August 1, 1983. A three-week "vacation peace assembly" was held and by August 19 the number present was 200. But it was difficult to keep that many in Israel. Since local Israelis constituted only 65 of the 200, the others had to come from elsewhere, at considerable cost for travel and time lost from work. A plea was sent out for reinforcements. The number meeting in Jerusalem rose but kept falling back. It was never below 100, but the ups and downs were considerable. Therefore the experiment was ended on September 30.

But the fluctuations had one advantage: the variations in the effect of the group could be very finely tracked with the variations on the statistical indexes. Of course, ordinarily one would have to worry that something like weekends or weather trends would cause both the numbers gathering and the national statistics to vary together. But thanks to the time series analysis technique, which systematically examines these possible contaminations of the results, any effects of such trends or patterns can be identified.

Unlike the other three cases described in the last chapter, the social scientists were on the scene well ahead of time to plan their research strategy for Israel. Drs. Charles "Skip" Alexander from Harvard and David Orme-Johnson came to Israel to put together an "Index of National Progress." It was based on statistics routinely gathered by the government and felt by scientists to be the most relevant and reliable for indicating an improvement in national life. The two researchers refined their index with Israeli scientists, then lodged their predictions months in advance with independent review boards in Israel and the United States.

What were the measures and the results? The analysis is still in progress, but the results so far indicate the following:

War deaths in Lebanon averaged 28 per day when the numbers practicing the TM-Sidhis together in Jerusalem fell below the "threshold" of 200; the average was one per day during the seven times the number was above 200.(see fig. 8.1)

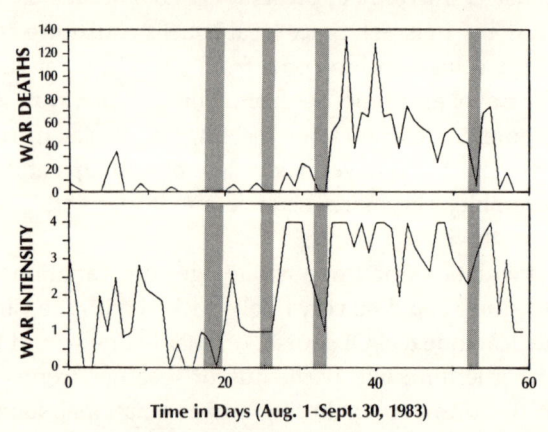

Fig. 8.1. War deaths and war intensity levels in Lebanon during period of Israel experiment, showing (in shaded areas) times in which the number of advanced experiencers of pure consciousness meditating together exceeded the predicted critical number of 200. (Based on data in preliminary report of [1].)

The intensity of fighting in Lebanon on a given day was also strongly associated with the number meeting in Jerusalem — more meeting on a given day, less intensity.

Accidental fires, illegal fires, total fires, and all other disorderly events dealt with by the fire department — same association of higher numbers with fewer incidents.

Auto accidents in Jerusalem — same association.

Israeli stock market, considered a measure of the country's confidence in its own future, went up when the numbers were up, down when the numbers were down.

If the question of causality still lingers

The general level of positive feeling reflected in the front page picture story of the newspaper, as measured by the same type of analysis described in Chapter 6, in which the raters did not know the relation between the news and the numbers meeting — same association of more positivity when the numbers were up, less when they were down.

Lower temperatures in Jerusalem (since this was summer time, that means better weather) — same association.

Accuracy of weather predictions in the Jerusalem area — when numbers were up, accuracy was greater.

Mood of taxi drivers — not statistically analyzed, but intuition said this association was strongest of all!

The method of analysis was a "multivariate state space forecasting system" — basically a fancy time series analysis. Each of these statistics was plotted by a computer so as to show the trends and cycles existing in the past, and a formula was derived for describing a "model" of how that statistic was likely to act on any given day in the future (taking into account any noticeable patterns, like changes that occur on weekends). Then that was used to predict the daily levels between August 15 and September 30.

Next, a similar equation was developed that included the daily number meeting in Jerusalem. If this latter formula was much better at predicting the statistic's level on any particular day, having 200 meeting in Jerusalem did have an effect.

This "intervention model" turned out to be an extraordinary predictor of every statistic. For example, it predicted intensity of fighting in Lebanon several hundred times more accurately than the model based only on previous trends. When the number was high, the fighting was sure to be less intense — and the taxi drivers more cheerful.

The tight relation between this set of statistics as a whole and the number meeting in Jerusalem is very striking (see fig. 8.2).

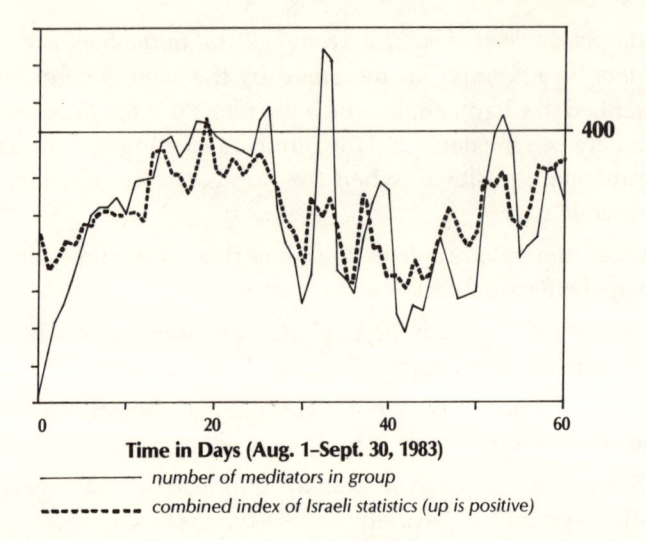

Fig. 8.2. Average of major Israeli statistical indicators (adjusted so that up means positive in each case) and number of advanced experiencers of pure consciousness meditating together during period of Israel experiment. (Based on data in preliminary report of [1].)

Perhaps even more impressive is the way all these diverse factors were obviously being affected by a single underlying influence. The same phenomenon was seen with the twenty-one Rhode Island statistics and the two Holland statistics. But here it was even clearer. When the numbers in Jerusalem (the single influence on them all) declined below the necessary threshold of 200, the factors did not behave "as one" (although their average did go down). What had been influencing them as a unit was apparently gone. Let's look at that in more detail.

When Orme-Johnson and Alexander statistically boiled the data down, three distinct groups of statistics emerged: war intensity/negative national feelings; stock market-related factors; and fire/temperature factors. In the past, and during the below-200 periods of this study, these three were completely unrelated to each other — when one improved, another might improve or not. But when 200 or more gathered in Jerusalem, these three factors moved as if they were one measure. Orme-Johnson and Alexander likened this to the way we hear a signal. When the signal — in this case, the effect of the number experiencing pure consciousness — is strong, then the noise from other things in the environment can't interfere with it much. Since turning up the volume on a vague or imaginary signal may prove it to have been only an illusion, this is a strong test for a real influence. In this case, no one had imagined anything. The signal was loud and clear.

The researchers themselves concluded:

> The purpose of employing experimental procedures is to attempt to control for alternative explanations other than those provided by the experimenter's hypothesis for the outcomes observed. In this case, the predicted and observed pattern of outcomes is so highly improbable that to even conceive of an alternative explanation becomes extremely difficult.[1]

But just in case your mind is buzzing with wild alternatives with which to challenge the scientists, let's consider yet another study.

Washington, D.C.

If you had to choose one place from which to influence the United States and also, indirectly, as much of the world as possible, you would pick the District of Columbia. Coming to the same conclusion, meditators agreed in 1982 that any who were interested and able to do so would move to Washington, D.C., to live there permanently and bring a little coherence to the city which controls the fate of so many people in so many lands.

Their goal was to establish a group of 400. The square-root-of-

1% formula said only 173 ought to be needed. But it was felt that as the national capital, Washington was definitely "bigger" in some sense and in need of extra numbers "for insurance."

Prior to early 1983 the number of advanced experiencers of pure consciousness meditating together in Washington was rarely more than 40 or 50. But by May 1983 the number was suddenly fluctuating around 400.

This was a research opportunity that did not go unnoticed by Audrey Lanford, a Stanford Ph.D. who had been in Washington for several years, teaching sociology at Catholic University. In 1983 she began doing full-time research on collective consciousness, including the pair of landmark studies we are about to describe. Both looked at the effects of pure consciousness on the quality of life in Washington — one focusing on the homicide rate[2] and the other on stock prices of Washington-based companies[3].

Homicide was selected as a measure of community incoherence for two reasons. First, unlike some crime rates, it is not influenced very much by changes in law enforcement practices. That is, it seems to be a deep measure of community coherence. According to the FBI, "It has long been recognized that murder is a primarily societal problem over which law enforcement has little or no control."[4] Second, homicides are almost always reported to the police, making police homicide data the most reliable of all measures of criminal or violent activity.

Lanford obtained homicide statistics from the District of Columbia Metropolitan Police for August 1980 through November 1983 and computed weekly totals for the 173 weeks of this period. Using that dear statistical tool, the time series analysis, Lanford then removed all cyclical trends (such as seasonal and monthly changes). Then she compared the weeks in which the numbers in the groups meeting together were greater than 400 on at least one day (there were 38 such weeks) to the weeks in which there

wasn't a single day when the critical number of 400 was reached.*
(The first time they reached 400 was in June 1982, but the numbers did not reach 400 very often until mid-May 1983.)

The results? The weeks with 400 had 22% fewer homicides, a difference "statistically significant at the .02 level." This means that the probability of getting this large a change in homicide rate merely by chance is less than two in a hundred. As for the 22% reduction, for the citizens of Washington this meant approximately one less homicide per week during the over-400 weeks. Lanford emphasizes that the weeks in which there were more than 400 meditators bore no systematic relation to any other events and were essentially randomly distributed. In her research report she exhaustively analyzed other potential causes for a decrease in homicide: for example, changes in police coverage, weather, citizen prevention activities, and population shifts. In each case, either there was no significant change in the factor over the period of the study, or the changes did not occur in any consistent relation to the over-400 weeks.

Lanford's second study looked at the other side of community coherence — its strengths. In this case, she looked at its economic strength, and specifically the strength of Washington-based companies compared to other U.S. companies. To do this she used the Johnston-Lemon stock index, which computes average daily

---

*Lanford also attempted an analysis comparing the weeks with and without 173. However, she had to abandon the analysis because she found that before mid-1983 there were very few times this number was reached, and after this time it was reached every week. There were indeed fewer homicides during the weeks in which the number was over 173—the number needed according to the square-root-of-1% formula. But because there was simply a before-versus-after distribution of weeks, it was not possible to do the proper statistical analysis. She also compared weeks with four days at the 400 level to weeks with no days. These results were the same as what we're about to report.

closing prices of thirty stocks of Washington-based companies and is published daily in the Washington *Post*.

Her analysis was based on weekly averages beginning July 13, 1981 (the first day on which the Johnston-Lemon index was publicly available) through September 30, 1983 (when she completed the study). Again a time series analysis was used to remove the effects of any cyclical or other trends. And again the results were clear: stock prices were substantially higher during the weeks when more than 400 were practicing together. The "level of significance" indicated that the odds of this happening by chance were "less than .001" — a very strong result.

What About These Studies?

At this point it becomes very difficult to think of anything that could be causing these changes in war deaths, fires, accidents, crime, stock market prices, and the like except the changes in the numbers in these groups. Still, you may be thinking that maybe whatever makes people go to the group to meditate on those days (cooler weather in Jerusalem) is also what makes people buy stocks and not commit homicide. It is true that the days on which the large groups met were not randomly chosen. But the time series analysis in both studies found no regular, prior trends that could not be statistically eliminated in their effects on the analysis. In D.C., weather variations were unrelated to the over-400 weeks. (In Israel, weather was an "outcome," but good weather had not affected stock prices, crime rate, etc., in the past.) If there was a factor, it would have had to have been one which had not existed until the large groups were meeting, one which fluctuated very closely with the numbers in the groups. It is hard to imagine what such a factor could be, except the groups themselves.

Still, if you would like a study in which the decision to come and be in these groups was not left up to the people involved, we did a small study of this type in Atlanta, Georgia, in which we moved groups of advanced meditators into and out of high crime areas for four completely arbitrary one- or two-week periods over which the participants had no control.[5, 6] A "pilot study" is social science jargon for a study that tests certain ideas on a small scale before investing time and money on a large study. In this case, the numbers of advanced meditators (28 to 40) were never enough to affect all of Atlanta. Therefore, they had to be moved from area to area, improving one section of the city while detracting from the one they'd left — a very poor approach to social change. But the study does fill in that possible gap in the causality issue. It also solves one we hadn't raised — there was never any advanced publicity or public knowledge of these experiments. In this pilot study violent crimes dropped 10% to 30% each time the group was in the high crime area, and rose 10% to 30% in the area where they formerly met — an effect that was reversed when they returned to their original locale.*

Now you may be thinking, "Yes, but if we could just see some real, objective change in a *person* in one of these affected areas, and not just a change in a 'rate.'"

Another pilot study[7] found just such a change. In the next chapter we will describe the effect of the first U.S. gathering that was large enough (1,600 or more) to influence the entire country. It occurred in Amherst, Massachusetts, in the summer of 1979, when 2,500 advanced meditators met for several weeks. During that time David Orme-Johnson used people meditating in Iowa — 1,170 miles from Amherst — to "detect" the coherence in the

---

*A "pilot study" is social science jargon for a study that tests certain ideas on a small scale before investing time and money on a large study. In this case, the numbers of advanced meditators (28 to 40) were never enough to affect all of Atlanta. Therefore, they had to be moved from area to area, improving one section of the city while detracting from the one they'd left—a very poor approach to social change. But the study does fill in that possible gap in the causality issue. It also solves one we hadn't raised—there was never any advanced publicity or public knowledge of these experiments.

social field that the Amherst group was supposed to be creating.

Specifically, he and his associates looked at the EEG or brain waves of three Iowa subjects. Each was alone in a sound-shielded room and unaware of the purpose of the experiment. Also, the laboratory technicians, who did know the study's purpose, were kept unaware of when the group in Amherst would be meditating. On top of that, Orme-Johnson had everyone routinely remove their watches, and had set the laboratory clocks slightly off.

The three subjects meditated three times when the Amherst group was meditating, three times when it was not, and then again in September after the Amherst meeting was over. When the results appeared in the *International Journal of Neuroscience*, they were clear and surprising: during the crucial times in Amherst, EEG coherence did not increase in the meditators themselves, but it did increase among the three persons, even though they were in separate rooms. That is, their brains all reflected a pattern of functioning that was very similar to each other's. It was a physiological measure of exactly what was described in Chapter 5 — a field effect such that when a wave passed through, "all the corks on the pond bobbed together." At other times, the three still evidenced EEG coherence, but it was only coherence among various parts of their own brain except when the group in Amherst was meditating.

By now we think you should be fairly impressed. The Israel and Washington, D.C. studies explore the issue of causality in a new and powerful way. The Maharishi Effect behaved like a classic scientific law. You probably remember those simple laws from your high school science lab. For example, when the temperature rises in a balloon, the gas expands and the balloon gets bigger. When the temperature declines, the gas contracts and the balloon gets smaller. Now you know a new law — when more people experience pure consciousness together, the coherence in the social field increases and the crime rate goes down. When fewer people experience pure consciousness together, the coherence decreases and the crime rate goes up.

Actually, few scientific "laws" — especially social ones — are this consistent in their effects unless they are very, very powerful. Children don't always imitate their elders, prices don't always go up when there is a shortage. In the case of crimes or stock purchases, many factors interact to produce the final action. For this reason the *consistency* of the Maharishi Effect on behavior is quite dramatic.

However, you still may want to see some truly practical, large-scale results — like improving an entire large nation. And you have a right to prefer that the affected nation be one of the two "superpowers" who are endangering our species. Or perhaps you are thinking, "How nice, a few isolated, affluent areas of the word are improved, while the whole world teeters on the brink." In the next chapter the social effects of the experience of pure consciousness finally demonstrates its real purpose, its full dignity, its vital importance — when we describe what happened when the necessary 1,600 began meeting repeatedly in the United States, and when the necessary 7,000 first met to affect the world.

9

A World of Difference

It's worth the detour. If you are ever driving across Iowa on I-80, get off at Iowa City and drive south about an hour to Fairfield. The rolling hills are all soybeans and corn in summer, snow and hogs in winter. Every rise has its attractive farm and every ravine has its stream and woods. It is quite pretty, but a bit predictable by the time you get to Fairfield.

From a distance you see the town's church spires and the courthouse and trees and the grain elevators. You go under the Burlington Northern Railway underpass. And to your left you see not one, but two enormous, low, gold-colored domes.

Some people think they are seeing space ships from another planet. They are almost right — we could say these are "inner space ships" for guiding this planet to safety. They were built to hold enough advanced experiencers of pure consciousness to spread coherence to every corner of the globe.

Besides these domes, there are numerous other buildings, all adding up to what looks like a typical small, midwestern university, which, except for its domes, is pretty much was it is. In 1974 a group of young Ph.D.'s practicing the TM program moved to the then-empty college campus (to which "golden domes" were later added). These professors were determined to create a new kind of university, one where students and faculty and administration and janitors and cooks and purchasers would all meditate morning and evening. In other words, in this community, everyone would be growing in self-knowledge, especially the students. Not only would they be gaining knowledge in all the traditional fields, but they would be "expanding the container of knowledge" through the experience of pure consciousness. The faculty named their university Maharishi International University. They planned from the beginning to really *be* international, with branch campuses all over the world and a multinational student body.

The idea worked. Students came from the United States and abroad, including a contingent from China. IQs went up the longer students studied at M.I.U.[1], as compared to the usual pattern of small decreases beginning at this age. (Admissions are open. Physics and calculus are required. When students fail a class, it is assumed that after a few more months of meditating, they will be able to pass it, which they do.) The college gained accreditation, its graduates began going on to excellent graduate schools. Master's and doctoral programs were introduced and accredited, and a community of meditators took root in and around the campus.

Thus, eventually, the social scientists began to have a heavy case of the "what ifs" about this place. "What if the community contained enough people so that 1,600 would meditate together every morning and evening? Would that many permanently affect the whole country?" And then they really dreamed — "What if 7,000 of them lived there? Seven thousand might affect the whole planet. What would the world be like?"

After the gathering in Amherst in 1979, it was decided that

those free to do so might do their nation a great service if they could move to Fairfield, either to work towards a degree, join the faculty, start a business, or take a job.

People did move and are still moving. The little town of Fairfield was somewhat stunned by the first influx. But all in all, it has been an economic and cultural boon to southeast Iowa. To the natives, the new folks seem a bit strange but all right. If they seemed different at first, it was probably as much because the newcomers are usually from the urban coasts and that they have come to "spread coherence." Still, the reaction has been predictable: "They think they're going to change the world. But they're just ordinary folks!"

Just ordinary folks — doctors, carpenters, lawyers, restaurant owners, stock brokers, jewelers, real estate agents, novelists, appliance repairpersons, plus the students and faculty of the university. But every morning they go into their two golden domes for about an hour to "enliven the unified field." They come out around nine and go off to work or class, laughing and talking and making plans and deals with each other like "ordinary folks." In the evening they come back again. And again the next morning, and again the next evening, and again and again, day in and day out, morning and evening, in snow or rain, through freezing winds or tempting sunshine.

These people are determined to perform what to them is a crucial experiment. Their hope is very literally to rescue the world — and their nation, and themselves. They don't dwell on the thought, but the awareness of the threat of nuclear war is as much with them as with us all. But more than that, they want to create something much better, something that will last. They don't have any specific goals or feel that everyone should act or think or feel a certain way. They believe simply that the obviously abundant human traits of coherence, intelligence, creativity, harmony, love, health, and broad awareness can prevail, and that experiments so far indicate that their experience of pure consciousness as a group can bring out those latent qualities in the social field. How have they done?

Sixteen Hundred Citizens Change Their Nation

In 1982 and early 1983 the numbers of people practicing the TM and Tm-Sidhi program together in Fairfield fluctuated near a population of 1,600. (It is now almost always well over 1,600.) Many of these people were students who went home for vacations. Others were visitors who came and went. Some had moved to Fairfield permanently but had to travel at times because of their professions. In all, a population of 1,600 was achieved on five different occasions over this period. During each of these there were noticeable improvements in the nation and the world.[2, 3, 4]

The Effect on the Stock Market

Perhaps the most dramatic and visible effect has not been on some high spiritual plane, but on the Dow Jones industrial average! The stock market is probably not the ultimate measure of a nation's well-being, but it does indicate confidence and economic strength. Furthermore, since 1945, a rise in the stock market has always preceded recovery from an economic recession.

Beginning in March 1982, all the stable growth in the stock market occurred during or immediately after high numbers were reported in Fairfield (see fig. 9.1). Sudden rises in the numbers there were always followed by rises in the Dow Jones. During each seven-day period following a peak level in Fairfield, the average rise of the stock market was forty-seven times greater than the rest of the year. A time series analysis of daily fluctuations made it very clear that other cycles and trends were not the cause of these rises in the Dow Jones.

A world of difference

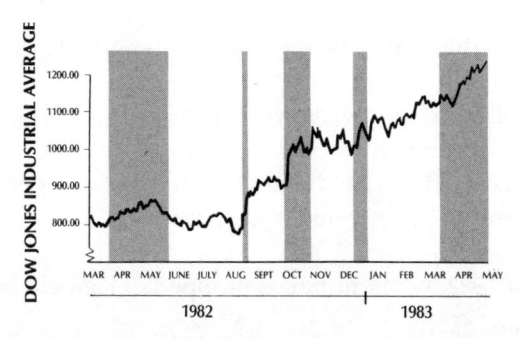

Fig. 9.1. Dow Jones industrial average from March 1982 through May 1983 noting periods in which number of advanced experiencers of pure consciousness meditating together exceeded the critical number of 1,600 predicted to affect the entire United States. (Based on data in [4].)

The Effect on Just About Everything Else

A separate time series analysis[2] found a strong, statistically significant decline in traffic deaths in the United States following those days when 1,600 meditated together in Fairfield.

Other results, not analyzed as extensively, are listed below:

1. During the first period when 1,600 was reached, in late March and early April 1982 —
   - Monthly inflation was the lowest in four years.
   - There were peaceful elections in El Salvador.
   - U.S. stock market rallied despite pessimistic forecasts.

2. During the second period, in mid-August 1982 —
   - Records were set on Wall Street.
   - Federal Reserve discount rate was cut to 10%.
   - Important bipartisan action was taken on a tax bill in Congress.
   - President Reagan called it the "most rewarding and fulfilling week" of his presidency.
   - Fighting stopped in Lebanon.

3. During the third such period (October and early November 1982) —
   - U.S. dollar rose to twelve-year high.
   - Personal income in U. S. rose .7%.
   - India and Pakistan held first friendly talks in a decade.
   - China and U.S.S.R. sought to restore ties.

4. December 1982, when numbers dropped in Fairfield but 2,000 met in Italy —
   - U.S. dollar dropped and European currencies improved!
   - Martial law was lifted in Poland.
   - Talks began on withdrawing foreign forces from Lebanon.
   - U.S.S.R. and U.S. proposed nuclear arms reductions.

5. Early April 1983 —
   - U.S. stock market reached record highs (this time predicted in advance by Maharishi Effect researchers) and the market was up an unprecedented eight days in a row.
   - U.S. industrial production was up 2.1%, the biggest increase in eight years.
   - Personal income rose .8%.
   - U.S. consumer confidence was the highest ever recorded.
   - Major social security legislation passed and was called "a victory for bipartisan cooperation."
   - U.S. expressed unexpected willingness to negotiate grain agreement with U.S.S.R.

Looking at the year of 1982 as a whole:

- Crime went down 4% — the first drop in twenty years. That translates into 1,576 fewer murders; 40,189 fewer robberies; and 373,980 fewer burglaries.
- Drug abuse declined (6%) for the first time.

A world of difference

- Traffic fatalities were down 10.7% — to the lowest rate in the nation's history.
- SAT scores went up for the first time in fourteen years.
- Divorce rate declined 4.5% (51,772 fewer broken homes) — the first decline in twenty years.
- Infant mortality declined 4% — to the lowest rate ever.
- Accidental death rate declined 6%.
- Alcohol consumption decreased 5%.
- Cigarette smoking decreased 2.5%.
- Hospital admissions decreased 3.9%.
- The average life expectancy rose in 1982 from 74.1 to 74.5 years.
- Productivity per acre and milk per cow were both at all time highs. Honey production rose 18%.
- Leading economic indicators rose seven months in a row (September 1982 to March 1983).
- In a Gallup poll in six diverse countries, the majority of those polled said they liked the people of the United States and almost all agreed U.S. influence on the world was growing.

The effect on the first months of 1983:

- GNP increased 5.8%.
- Stock indices rose 16.5% for first quarter of 1983.
- A survey by the American Medical Association found a 4.7% decline in visits to doctors.
- National productivity in the nonfarm sector rose 4.4%, the largest increase in two years. Factory worker productivity rose 8.3%.
- Wholesale prices dropped, the first decline since 1952.
- Consumer prices increased only .1% in March — the lowest single-month increase in eighteen years — making the econ-

omy inflation-free for five months.
- Seasonally adjusted unemployment dropped .6%.

And When There Weren't Sixteen Hundred —

1. June and July of 1982 —
   - War in the Falklands.
   - Invasion of Lebanon, bombing of Beirut.
   - Escalation of Iran-Iraq war.

2. September 1982 —
   - Fighting renewed in Lebanon; a Beirut massacre.
   - Rioting in Poland.

3. Late November 1982 —
   - Civil violence in Washington, D.C.

4. Mid-April 1983 —
   - Bombing of the U.S. Embassy in Beirut.

5. Early May 1983 —
   - Tornadoes in United States.
   - Rioting in Poland.

But Overall, a Sustained Rise

In spite of the above dips in events (mostly world events), 1982 through 1984 saw an impressive, sustained improvement in U.S. quality of life on many levels. No other period in our history has seen all these factors improve simultaneously. Social problems have certainly not been completely solved, but the country evidences a remarkable balance of overall enthusiasm and unity with an orderly redressing of unacceptable tendencies as they arise or receive public attention. The major area of difficulty for the

United States is still world events. But 1,600 are not enough to affect the world. Before we broach that topic, however, we will briefly describe one other study — of the one time prior to 1982 that 1,600 or more met in one place in the United States.

The Amherst Breakthrough

The Amherst meeting was held from July 9 to August 20, 1979 and brought together 2,500. Since this well exceeded the 1,600 predicted to be necessary to affect the United States, J. L. Davies and Skip Alexander were eager to study the effect on national statistics. They were both working in the Department of Psychology and Social Relations at Harvard at the time, and before the gathering they chose some national statistics to watch. These were violent crimes, plus death by various sudden causes — auto accidents, suicide, air accidents, and all other accidents.

Unfortunately, many of these statistics are reported monthly, so Davies and Alexander[5] used data for the six weeks of the Amherst gathering when possible, but otherwise used data from the months of July and August 1979. To have something to compare to, they computed the expected level of violent crime and sudden deaths for those months (if the meeting in Amherst had not happened). It was calculated by averaging the rates for the same period in 1973 through 1978, skipping 1979 of course, and including 1980 and 1981 when these became available.

The results? There was a decline for every statistic: violent crimes, including murder and homicide, and all nineteen kinds of accidents except drowning and three other very minor categories in August only. Also unaffected were water transport accidents in both months. But this actually emphasized the role of the meeting in Amherst, since most water transport deaths occurred too far out at sea for the Amherst gathering to have affected them. Similarly, the declines in crime and deaths seen throughout the continental United States were not seen in Hawaii and Alaska.

In most cases the level during the meeting was the lowest level of that statistic for any July or August between 1973 and 1981. Overall, the average decline on all statistics was "statistically significant at the .002 level."

Seven Thousand World Citizens Seek to Help Their Planet

You've probably forgotten how bad things were in the fall of 1983. We all seem to be blessed with short memories for fear. But there was plenty of cause for anxiety. Soviet-U.S. relations were at an all-time, terrifying low. The arms talks had ended in a tantrum. Many had watched "The Day After" on TV and then discussed it and dreamed it for weeks. The United States had "intervened" in Grenada. "Peacekeeping forces" by the hundreds were being killed in Lebanon. Central America continued to throb and divide opinions throughout the hemisphere.

The winter holidays of peace and light had never seemed so poignantly important, if futile. Then, on top of everything else, most of the United States got horribly cold.

And to the heart of the cold, 7,000 people came. They came from all fifty states, and from sixty countries as well, to Fairfield, Iowa, on six weeks' notice, to spend their holidays applying their approach to the world situation. Two hundred mobile homes and a huge prefab building had to be erected to feed and house them all and to let them meet in one place. The Minnesota company that agreed to do it felt their accomplishment — the biggest (60,000 sq. ft.), fastest (three weeks) prefab ever — was nothing short of a miracle.

But the miracles had only started —

The weather got warmer.

The stock market rose *throughout the world*[6], both as shown by change in the World Stock Index (fig. 9.2), and by simultaneous

A world of difference

increases in all of the major industrialized, capitalist countries (fig. 9.3).

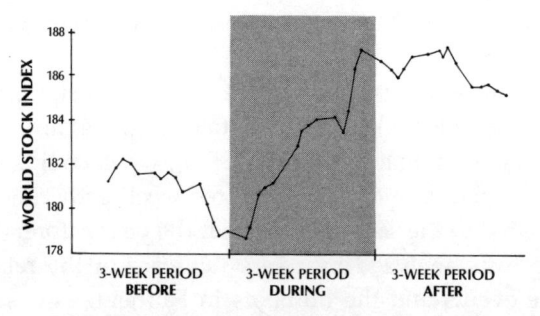

Fig. 9.2. World Stock Index (Capital International S. A., Geneva) over three weeks before, during, and after period in which number of advanced experiencers of pure consciousness meditating together exceeded critical number of 7,000 predicted to affect the entire world. (Based on data in preliminary report of [6].)

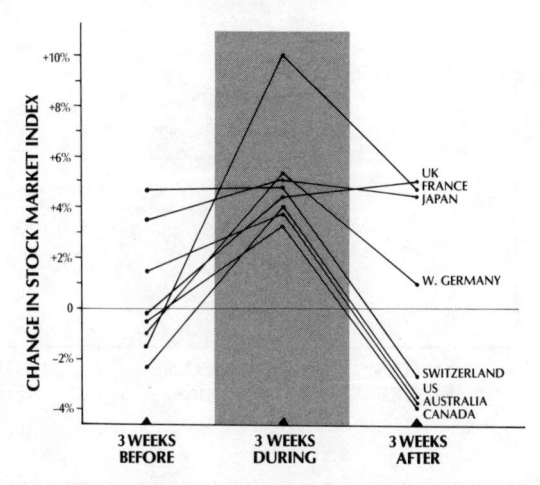

Fig. 9.3. Percentage change in major stock market indices over three weeks before, during, and after period in which number of advanced experiencers of pure consciousness meditating together exceeded critical number of 7,000 predicted to affect the entire world. (Based on data from preliminary report of [6].)

During the three-week period, worldwide air traffic fatalities were 49% lower than the average for the previous five years for the same dates, and 29% lower than the lowest figure for any of those five years.

A systematic analysis of news events[7] found sharp increases in positive statements by heads of states (fig. 9.4) and decreases in level of international conflicts (fig. 9.5), when compared to the three weeks before and after the three-week gathering of 7,000 and compared to the same time of year the year before. (The *New York Times* was analyzed by raters unaware of the relation between the events and the numbers in Fairfield, as described in Chapter 6). A few of these events are listed below.

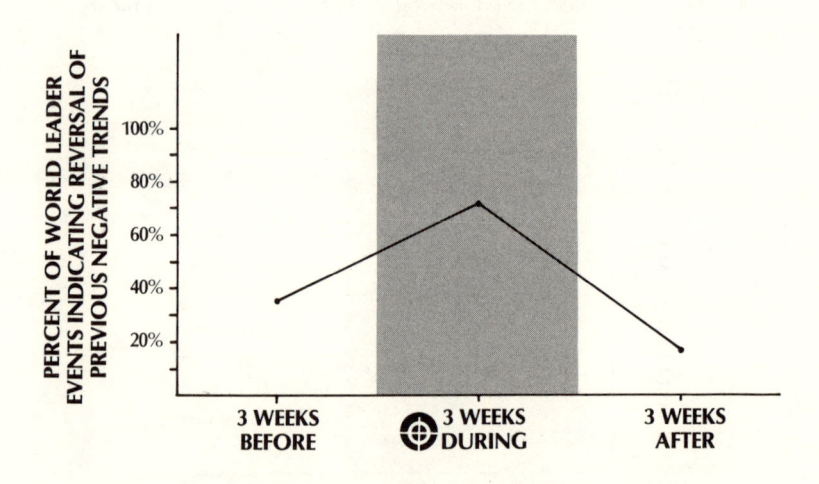

Fig. 9.4. Percentage of world leader events indicating reversal of prior negative trends (based on content analysis of *New York Times*) over three weeks before, during, and after period in which number of advanced experiencers of pure consciousness meditating together exceeded critical number of 7,000 predicted to affect the entire world. (Based on data from preliminary report of [7].)

A world of difference

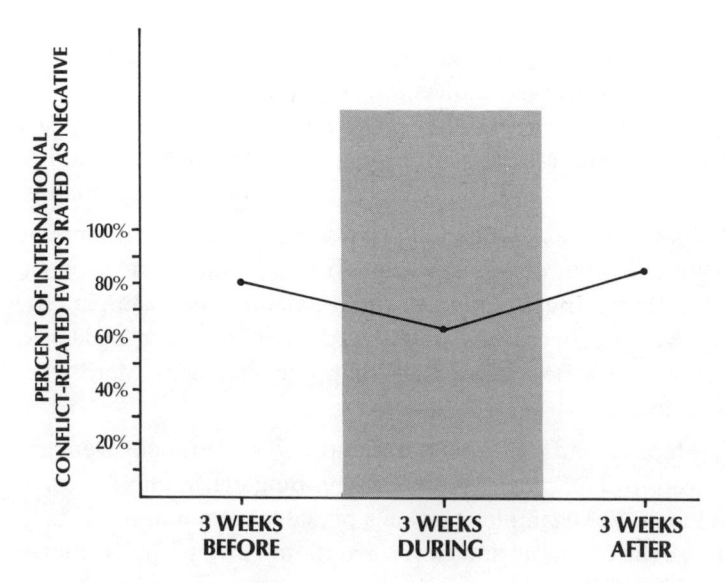

Fig. 9.5. Percentage of events in situations of international conflicts rated as negative (based on content analysis of *New York Times*) over three weeks before, during, and after period in which number of advanced experiencers of pure consciousness meditating together exceeded critical number of 7,000 predicted to affect the entire world. (Based on data from preliminary report of [7].)

1. Reports of efforts to ease internal political strife and disunity came from Ireland, Malta, Turkey, Cyprus, Israel, Chad, Sri Lanka, Japan, Argentina, and Canada. For example, local press in Cypress reported a "peace wave," and there were peaceful elections in India and Bangladesh (for the latter, the first elections in seven years). One of Argentina's militant groups announced it would disband, renounce violence, and pursue becoming a legal political party, and the Argentine government met with human rights organizations for the first time since 1976. The president of Sri Lanka "extended the olive branch" to opposition parties. The Japanese prime minister united a divided party and pledged to end corruption.

2. Leaders of the United States, Soviet Union, China, and many other countries emphasized peace. Ireland's politicians announced a first — a united effort to bring peace to Ulster. Peace talks in Lebanon resulted in a formal agreement between all rival groups to halt fighting in Beirut and the surrounding mountains.

3. Freedom was granted or promised to political prisoners by the governments of Mozambique, Tunisia, Zimbabwe, Angola, South Korea, the Philippines, and Poland. For example, the South Korean government announced it would release 1,600 prisoners under a new amnesty. Philippine President Marcos released 280.

4. Steps to end corruption and improve government were announced in the Soviet Union, Turkey, Bulgaria, Zambia, China, and Japan. For example, Zambia's president announced plans to stabilize the economy and stop corruption. Turkey's prime minister proposed to streamline its government and invigorate the economy, then won a vote of confidence.

5. Major education reforms were announced or initiated in Great Britain, the Soviet Union, and the United States.

6. Improved relations through talks, treaties, pronouncements, etc. were reported between thirty-two countries. For example, East and West German relations "seem to be brighter than for many years" after "extraordinary momentum in strengthening links" (London *Times*, December 29, 1983). There was a marked improvement in talks between Angola and Mozambique.

7. New recognition of the rights of minorities was made in Hungary, Egypt, Israel, Iraq, Uganda, and Sri Lanka. For example, the Ugandan government announced it would allow several thousand ethnic Rwandans to return to their homes.

Of course, one can always find some examples of good news in the *New York Times*. But these are examples from a careful tabulation of all world news, which found a dramatic and "statistically significant" change in the ratio of positive to negative events as shown in figure 9.5 on page 147.

In general, worldwide statistics are not easily obtained, nor is it feasible for researchers personally to gather statistics for every country in the world. Therefore, the following indicators were obtained from the United States and Australia (when possible), to see if the effect were being felt on opposite sides of the globe. Also, the results described here are from preliminary reports available as of the date of publication. Since governments are generally slow to compile their statistics, what could be gathered and reported right away was necessarily fragmentary.

1. U.S. traffic fatalities over the holidays were the lowest ever, even though miles driven were the highest ever. Available statistics in Australia (from Western Australia, New South Wales, and Victoria) showed a decline of about 10% compared to previous years.

2. There were fewer infectious diseases in the United States and Australia compared to the same weeks during the previous five years and to the periods immediately before and after (fig. 9.6 on page 150).

3. There were more patent applications in the United States and Australia compared to the same weeks during the previous five years and to the periods immediately before and after (fig. 9.7 on page 151).

4. A time series analysis of crime rates in the District of Columbia and in the state of Victoria in Australia (the only Australian government that responded to the researchers' request for statistics by the time of the study) found significant decreases during the three-week period that were not accounted for by cyclical or other trends.

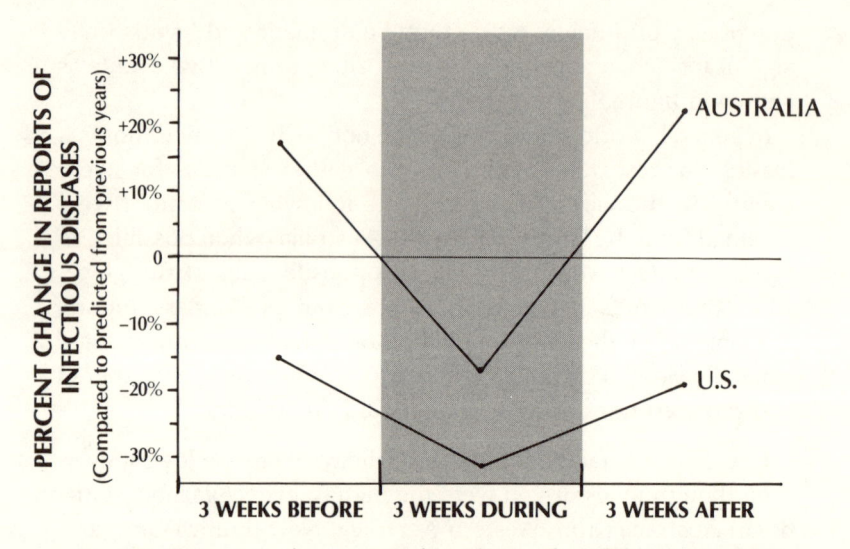

Fig. 9.6. Percentage change in total incidence of notifiable infectious diseases (compared to previous years) for the United States and Australia over three weeks before, during, and after period in which number of advanced experiencers of pure consciousness meditating together exceeded critical number of 7,000 predicted to affect the entire world. (Based on data in preliminary report of [7], which summarizes statistics from U.S. Center for Disease Control and Department of Health, Commonwealth of Australia.)

5. Finally, for the United States, Christmas buying rose 13%, to a five-year high, and there were no U.S. service deaths in Beirut. According to polls, by New Year's day there was an all time high in *optimism* in the United States (a few weeks after great pessimism — ah, those blessed short memories.) "Americans approach 1984 optimistically, feeling that . . . the near future will be significantly better." (*New York Times,* Jan. 1, 1984).

When the "Assembly of 7,000" broke up on January 6, the world felt different — safer, more optimistic. Unfortunately, if you look at the statistics for the three weeks before, during, and after, you see a major improvement during, but a return to those

A world of difference

earlier negative world events within three weeks after. The stock market also plummeted, infectious diseases rose again, patent applications dropped, and so forth. The obvious conclusion is that we need 7,000 some place permanently. It's that simple.

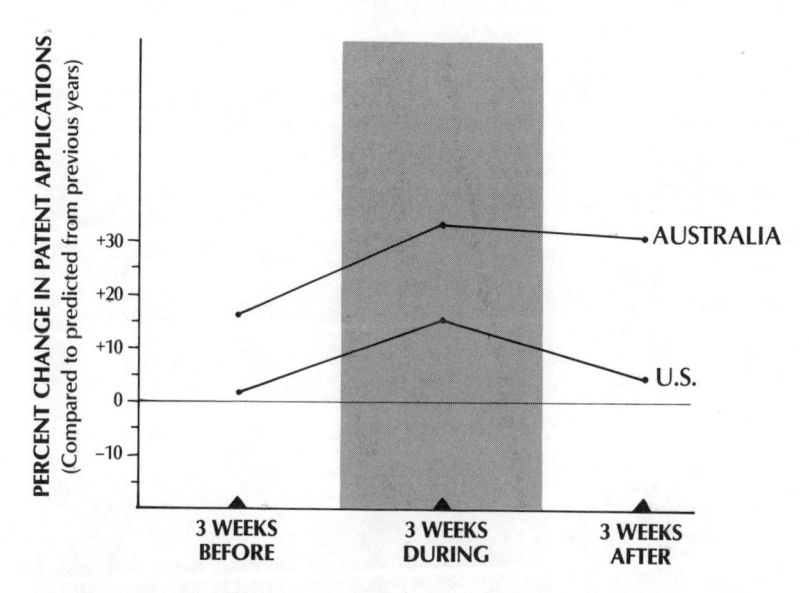

Fig. 9.7. Percentage change in number of patent applications compared to predicted number for the United States and Australia over three weeks before, during, and after period in which number of advanced experiencers of pure consciousness meditating together exceeded critical number of 7,000 predicted to affect the entire world. (Based on data in preliminary report of [7], which summarizes statistics from U.S. Patent Office and Australia Patent, Trade Marks and Design Office.)

10

What If It's All True?

We wonder what you are thinking now. Are you delighted? Full of optimism? Angry and frustrated that this approach has not been tried more often? Or are you still incredulous? Wondering if it's all a gimmick? Wondering what it means for you?

Optimism, frustration, incredulity — we've had *all* these feelings about this research and its applications. And we're guessing that your main question right now is —

How Can I Know for Sure This Is True?

In deciding whether this research has any validity, we have a major advantage over most of you in that we know the research so thoroughly. We are also specialists in research methods, having taught the subject for years and written texts about research methods. For us it is clear that this research is sound, in spite of our own strong, if irrational, doubts on some days that a few people meditating can really affect the whole world.

You have our sympathy in trying to sort out what you have read in this book. As we explained in Chapter 1, technically, in science, nothing is True for Sure. Scientists deal in probabilities. You've read what we have to say; now you may want to gather other opinions. But remember what we said about Type I and Type II errors — it might be better to err on the side of credulity in this case. And when you ask for other opinions, be aware that you may not always get an objective evaluation. See below.

If It's True, Shouldn't I Have Heard About It Before?

Yes, you should have. Except that newly discovered laws of nature (as opposed to fads in thinking about them) usually have to become well accepted by science before they become well known to the public. And scientists are humans too, with pride and prejudices. They don't want to come out in favor of something they believe can't exist.

At a convention we surveyed ninety psychologists about the pure consciousness experience (with no mention of any particular technique or tradition).[1] We asked them had they ever had it, did they know anyone who had, did they think it was worth studying, and if they were editor of a professional journal, would they recommend the publication of a study of pure consciousness. Among those polled, sixty-four (71%) had not had the experience. Of these, twenty-seven thought psychology should not study it and seventeen would not recommend the publication of a *sound* article about it. In fact, two of the "objective scientists" read the instructions and then tore up the questionnaire, making certain strong, unprintable statements as they threw it away!

It is probably understandable that scientists not having the pure consciousness experience would find it difficult to acknowledge its existence or encourage its study, given their generally mechanistic/materialistic/pre-quantum-physics assumptions. But scientists are part of their society and influenced by what society-at-large finds acceptable. So maybe the less mechanistic among us can encourage our scientist friends to be more open-minded.

In a similar vein, one complaint you may hear about the research in this book is that much of it is done by scientists who were meditators. That's true. But who else would do the research, regardless of the pay, the adequacy of the clerical help, the sophistication of the computers supplied, or all the other standard niceties paid for by research grants? In most countries researchers study what the government will fund them to study, and the government looks to the public for its reaction. One obvious suggestion is to let your government officials and representatives know you want research done on this topic. We'll return to this point.

Okay, Suppose I Accept It's True — What Would It Mean for Me Personally?

You Could Feel More Optimistic

For a start, you might begin feeling more hopeful about the future! We said in Chapter 3 that it seems our planet along with our species is going through some major transition, and rough as things are, it is natural that there should be some shakes and trembles as the old ship blasts into a new mode of moving. This is not a new idea — there are countless books on the subject, from Teilhard de Chardin and Buckminster Fuller to *The Global Brain* by Peter Russell and the ideas of Barbara Hubbard.

The basic prediction is that we are developing a new style of consciousness, a sort of global nervous system, a coherent and highly integrated collective consciousness. Just as multicellular life began with a few independent cells learning to cooperate and communicate as a whole, so we independent humans may soon recognize that we are part of a larger organism. The optimism comes from the thought that with this broader awareness of our oneness, we will treat each other and take care of our spaceship earth as we would our own self and body.

This book helps to change this basic prediction-cum-wishful-thinking into something resembling a reassuring scientific fact. If large groups of people continue to meet together to experience pure consciousness, and especially if these groups are permanent and number at least 7,000, we can infer from the research results reviewed in this book that crime, divorce, suicide, and accident rates should continue to drop, international tensions lessen, world war should continue to be unknown, arms agreements should be signed, military spending should lessen, the world's economy should improve, more international cooperation should be evidenced, poor countries should develop faster while maintaining their traditions better, environmental problems should be solved faster, alternative energies explored and applied at a greater rate — and you *personally* should notice more success in achieving your life's goals. Among other things.

Of course, optimism does not need to mean passivity. If the Maharishi Effect creates greater coherence, it means society will improve and individual people will make these improvements. Greater coherence in society means it will be easier for you to improve your world, and you will be more likely to choose to make the changes that will be best for everyone in the long run. A time of coherence is a time for more, not less, attention on improving society.

You Could Speed the Change

We've been implying that the change that is coming is almost inevitable. But it could be much faster and smoother if these large groups were permanently established. Delightful as it may be to live in a community of others who are experiencing pure consciousness, it isn't always easy to arrange. Only some people are free to move. And all of them need an income — hard to provide for 7,000 people in the Midwest. Or if the group is in a city, such as Washington, D.C., the problem becomes housing for 7,000 people of varying incomes in one area that is also close to jobs.

In comparison to the defense budgets of most governments (or the money spent fighting crime and housing criminals), it would cost very little to help establish a community of 7,000 people. Or better still, to train 7,000 in an existing community. Fortunately, most governments are accustomed to supporting research into promising new ideas. Even the tightest government budgets allot millions to research, including social science research. No government can afford not to test out new ideas. Our representatives merely need to know, through letters and telegrams and phone calls, that it is your desire to have the social effects of pure consciousness implemented and, of course, further evaluated.

It may be difficult to convince a government to decrease its defense budget. The dangers may simply seem too great, both to those in the government and those in the public. But to try something as an experiment merely depends on enough people asking for that experiment.

For that matter, the establishment of 7,000 is within the financial means of many corporations and individuals. One person could do it — and probably earn a place in history. In the case of corporations, the money saved in one year due to increased international instability would establish such a community permanently.

The importance of speeding the hopefully inevitable evolution of our collective consciousness is not just pie-in-the-sky sociology. It is a matter with considerable moral implications and many practical consequences. How much suffering might have been prevented after 1978 if the World Peace Project could have been continued? Once one knows about a preventative, there is no excuse for not using it.

In spite of the way they speed change, larger numbers of people experiencing pure consciousness also seem to make change come smoother. All change means some stress, some tumult, some loss of the old and getting accustomed to the new. Even good fortune means change and tumult. A rise in the stock market puts stress on the traders as they rush to make decisions. A wedding, a vacation, a new and better home — they all arouse our physiology and tax our inner resources.[2] Not that we don't want changes, but especially in the case of social change, the smoother the better.

Of course, there is a risk that comes with this smoothness — that people will take smooth change for granted. They'll fail to associate it with the large groups of people experiencing pure consciousness. We will all have to be on guard to see that the real cause of our peaceful-though-rapidly-progressing world is valued and sustained. Besides whatever economic support they need, the 7,000 people living in these communities should receive our utmost respect and appreciation. Past habits may make it easy to be light or trivial or simply to forget about people making such a commitment. That needs to change.

After you punch through the sound barrier, it almost feels as if you aren't moving — until you hit an obstacle. To use a more serene analogy, the invisible sap of the tree is what gives it life. It is what creates and then maintains and unifies bark and branch and leaf while everything also grows. To keep the tree healthy, we have to appreciate the sap's role and take steps to see that the tree has water with which to make its sap. Similarly, pure consciousness may be what maintains the unity within collective consciousness in spite of rapid change. But it seems to require that we be aware of this role so that we keep a certain number of people experiencing pure consciousness. This experience of it somehow enlivens pure consciousness (or as we said in Chapter 5, the unified field) and spreads its main characteristic — coherence — throughout the social field.

You Could Do It Yourself

The experience of pure consciousness is, to say the least, pleasant and good for you as an individual. The subjective and objective evidence for this was discussed in the first two chapters. And if you were to live in an area where groups meet to meditate (Fairfield, Iowa; Washington, D.C.; and smaller groups in most of the world's large cities), it would bring those crucial totals that much higher.

Some Final Thoughts

We've made it together to the end. You've been patient. Or maybe you are desperate for solutions. We all are. And some of us get afraid that in our desperation we will latch on to one more illusion, be disappointed by one more medicine show. Maybe you can't take another flim-flam and don't want to risk accepting this new hope. Maybe you feel afraid that if people decide to change the world by closing their eyes, experiencing pure consciousness and making the social field more coherent, this will lull them into indifference or divert their energy from the real work that needs to be done. We truly understand these feelings.*

It's simply so poetically just and intuitively right that the solution would come from *inside*, since we have't found it outside. It's logical that the answers should come from *silence*, just as the noise becomes unbearable. And from *rest*, just as the stress begins to bury us. And from *ourselves*, just as we are about to destroy us.

---

*The research, however, suggests the opposite. Maslow found self-actualized people, for whom "transcendental" and "peak" experiences were common, were far more concerned about social justice and actively humanitarian.[3] Simlarly, those experiencing pure consciousness through the TM technique evidence growth in moral judgment.[4, 5, 6]

It's certainly clear that something fresh and new needs to be added to the old ways that aren't working. So maybe it's worth taking a chance.

The fundamental law of Western logic is called "The law of the excluded middle." It means things are either true or false, good or bad. A fundamental of Eastern logic is "the coexistence of opposites." It means the balance in the middle, the still point, is the only important reality. It's instructive that our planet is currently threatened by two colossal, essentially Western superpowers that are trying to exclude the middle and insist that the other side adopt their way of life. It makes good evolutionary sense that as we live in the shadow of our own guns, some of us are finally learning to make use of the power of the silence at the center.

This silence is *not* Western or Eastern (although the knowledge of the use of it was bound to be better preserved in one place than another). This silence of pure consciousness is simply the sound of a species evolving out of a tight spot, and perhaps, if you like the thought, into a fuller reflection of its Creator.

REFERENCES

(Many of the studies referred to throughout the book have been printed or reprinted in one of the volumes of *Scientific Research on the Transcendental Mediation and TM-Sidhi Program: Collected Papers*. Volume 1 is edited by D. W. Orme-Johnson and J. T. Farrow and was published in 1977 by MIU Press (Livingston Manor, NY). Volumes 2 through 4 are in press and should appear during 1986. They are edited by R. A. Chalmers, G. Clements, H. Schenkluhn, and M. Weinless and published by MIU Press (Vlodrop, the Netherlands). Papers in these works are cited as *CP*:1 through *CP*:4, according to the volume.)

CHAPTER 1

1. Peters, R. S., ed. *Brett's History of Psychology*. Cambridge, Massachusetts: M.I.T. Press, 1962.
2. Teresa of Avila. *The Life of Teresa of Jesus*. Garden City, New York: Image Books, 1960 (Original work published 1583).
3. Aranya, S. H. *Yoga Philosophy of Pantanjali*. Calcutta: Pooran Press, 1963.
4. Lame Deer, Jr., and R. Erdoes. Lame Deer, seeker of visions. In *American Indian Literature: An Anthology*, ed. A. R. Velie. Norman, OK: University of Oklahoma Press, 1979.
5. Farrow, J. T., and J. R. Hebert. Breath suspension during the Transcendental Meditation technique. *Psychosomatic Medicine* 44 (1982):133-153.
6. Shear, J., and K. Eppley. Factors influencing the effectiveness of meditation and relaxation techniques. Paper presented at the annual convention of the American Psychological Association, Toronto, August 1984. Also see references in Chapter 10.

7. Mitroff, I. J. *The Subjective Side of Science.* New York: Elsevier, 1974.
8. Wallace, R. K. The physiological effects of the Transcendental Meditation program: A proposed fourth major state of consciousness. Doctoral Dissertation, University of California at Los Angeles, 1970. Reprinted in *CP:*1.
9. Selye, H. Foreword to *TM: Discovering Inner Energy and Overcoming Stress,* ed. by H. H. Bloomfield, M. P. Cain, and D. T. Jaffee. New York: Delacorte, 1975.
10. Orme-Johnson, D. W. Autonomic stability and Transcendental Meditation. *Psychosomatic Medicine* 35 (1973):341-349. Reprinted in *CP:*1.
11. Wallace, R. K., M. C. Dillbeck, E. Jacobe, and B. Harrington. The effects of the Transcendental Meditation and TM-Sidhi program on the aging process. *International Journal of Neuroscience* 16 (1982):53-59.
12. Borland, C., and G. Landrith. Improved quality of city life through the Transcendental Meditation program: Decreased crime rate. In *CP:*1.
13. Bassin, A. Quoted in M. Geyelin, Can group meditation help cut crime? *St. Petersburg Times* (Jan. 3, 1982):1-B, 13-B.

CHAPTER 2

1. Bucke, R. M. *Cosmic Consciousness.* New York: Dutton, 1969 (Original work published 1901).
2. Jung, C. G. *Memories, Dreams and Reflections.* Edited by A. Jaffe, New York: Vintage, 1965.
3. Fechner, G. T. *Elemente der Psychophysik.* Leipzig: Breitkopf and Hartel, 1860.
4. Dhanaraj, V. H. Reduction in metabolic rate during the practice of the Transcendental Meditation technique. Doctoral dissertation, University of Alberta, Edmonton, 1973. Summary in *CP:*1.
5. Wallace, R. K. The physiological effects of the Transcendental Meditation program: A proposed fourth major state of consciousness. Doctoral Dissertation, University of California at Los Angeles, 1970. Reprinted in *CP:*1.
6. Wallace, R. K. Physiological effects of Transcendental Meditation. *Science* 167 (1970):1751-1754. Reprinted in *CP:*1.
7. Wallace, R. K., H. Benson, and A. F. Wilson. A wakeful hypometabolic physiological state. *American Journal of Physiology* 221 (1971):795-799. Reprinted in *CP:*1.

8. Farrow, J. T. and J. R. Hebert. Breath suspension during the Transcendental Meditation technique. *Psychosomatic Medicine* 44 (1982):133-153.
9. Corey, P. W. Airway conductance and oxygen consumption changes associated with practice of the Transcendental Meditation technique. In *CP*:1.
10. Jevning, R., A. F. Wilson, W. R. Smith, and M. R. Morton. Redistribution of blood flow in acute hypometabolic behavior. *American Journal of Physiology* 235 (1979):R89-R92. Reprinted in *CP*:2.
11. Goleman, D., and G. Schwartz. Meditation as an intervention in stress-reactivity. *Journal of Consulting and Clinical Psychology* 44 (1976):456-466.
12. Orme-Johnson, D. W. Autonomic stability and Transcendental Meditation. *Psychosomatic Medicine* 35 (1973):341-349. Reprinted in *CP*:1.
13. West, M. A. Changes in skin resistance in subjects resting, reading, listening to music, or practicing the Transcendental Meditation technique. In *CP*:1.
14. Sultan, S. E. A study of the ability of individuals trained in the Transcendental Meditation technique to achieve and maintain levels of physiological relaxation. Master's thesis, University of California, San Diego, 1975. Summary in *CP*:2.
15. Jevning, R., and A. F. Wilson. Altered red cell metabolism in TM. *Psychophysiology* 14 (1977):94. Reprinted in *CP*:2.
16. Bevan, A. J. W. Endocrine changes in Transcendental Meditation. *Clinical and Experimental Pharmacology and Physiology* 7 (1980):75-76.
17. Jevning, R., A. F. Wilson, and J. M. Davidson. Adrenocortical activity during meditation. *Hormones and Behavior* 10 (1978):54-60. Reprinted in *CP*:2.
18. Bujatti, M., and P. Riederer. Serotonin, noradrenaline, and dopamine metabolites in the Transcendental Meditation technique. *Journal of Neural Transmission* 39 (1976):257-267. Reprinted in *CP*:2.
19. Banquet, J. P. EEG and meditation. *Electroencepholography & Clinical Neurophysiology* 33 (1972):454. Reprinted in *CP*:1.
20. Banquet, J. P. Spectral analysis of the EEG in meditation. *Electroencepholography & Clinical Neurophysiology* 35 (1973):143-151. Reprinted in *CP*:1.
21. Banquet, J. P., and M. Sailhan. EEG analysis of spontaneous and induced states of consciousness. *Revue d'Electroencephalographie et de Neurophysiologie Clinique* 4 (1974):445-453. Reprinted in *CP*:1.
22. Dillbeck, M. C., and E. C. Bronson. Short-term longitudinal effects

of the Transcendental Meditation technique on EEG power and coherence. *International Journal of Neuroscience* 14 (1981):147-151.
23. Levine, P. H. The coherence spectral array (COSPAR) and its application to the studying of spatial ordering in the EEG. *Proceedings of the San Diego Biomedical Symposium* 15 (1976):237-247.
24. Stigsby, B., J. C. Rodenberg, and H. B. Moth. Electroencephalographic findings during mantra meditation (Transcendental Meditation) – A controlled, quantitative study of experienced meditators. *Electroencephalography & Clinical Neurophysiology* 51 (1981):434-442.
25. Farrow, J. T. Physiological changes associated with transcendental consciousness, the state of least excitation of consciousness. In *CP*:1.
26. Badawi, K., A. M. Rouzere, and D. Orme-Johnson. Electrophysiological changes during periods of respiratory suspension in the Transcendental Meditation technique. In *CP*:2.
27. Orme-Johnson, D. W., and E. T. Haynes. EEG phase coherence, pure consciousness, creativity, and TM-Sidhi experiences. *International Journal of Neuroscience* 13 (1981):211-217.
28. Warshal, D. Effects of the Transcendental Meditation technique on normal and Jendrassik reflex time. *Perceptual and Motor Skills* 51 (1980):95-98. Reprinted in *CP*:2.
29. West, M. A. Physiological effects of meditation: A longitudinal study. *British Journal of Social and Clinical Psychology* 18 (1979):219-226.
30. Banquet, J. P., J. C. Bourzeix, and N. Leseure. Potentiels evoques et etats de vigilance induits au cours d'epreuves de temps de reaction de choix. *Revue d'Electroencephalographie et de Neurophysiologie Clinique* 19 (1979):221-227.
31. McEvoy, T. M., L. R. Frumkin, and S. W. Harkins. Effects of meditation on brainstem auditory evoked potentials. *International Journal of Neuroscience* 10 (1980):165-170. Reprinted in *CP*:2.
32. Wandhofer, A., G. Kobal, and K. H. Plattig. Shortening of latencies of human auditory evoked potentials during the Transcendental Meditation technique. *Zeitschrift EEG-EMG* 7 (1976):99-103. Reprinted in *CP*:2.
33. Bennett, J. E., and J. Trinder. Hemispheric laterality and cognitive style association with Transcendental Meditation. *Psychophysiology* 14 (1976):293-296. Reprinted in *CP*:2.
34. Benson, H., B. A. Rosner, B. R. Marzetta, and H. P. Klemchuk. Decreased blood pressure in borderline hypertensive subjects who practiced meditation. *Journal of Chronic Disease* 27 (1974):163-171.
35. Benson, H., and R. K. Wallace. Decreased blood pressure in hyper-

tensive subjects who practiced meditation. *Circulation,* Supplement II 45-46 (1972):516. Reprinted in *CP*:1.

36. Blackwell, B., I. B. Hanenson, S. S. Bloomfield, H. G. Magenheim, S. I. Nidich, and P. Gartside. Effects of Transcendental Meditation on blood pressure: A controlled pilot experiment. *Journal of Psychosomatic Medicine* 37 (1975):86. Reprinted in *CP*:1.

37. Blackwell, B., S. Bloomfield, P. Gartside, A. Robinson, I. Hanenson, H. Magenheim, S. Nidich, and R. Zigler. Transcendental Meditation in hypertension. *The Lancet* (January 31, 1976):223-226. Reprinted in *CP*:2.

38. Cooper, M. J., and M. M. Aygen. Effect of meditation on serum cholesterol and blood pressure. *Journal of the Israel Medical Association* 95 (1978):1-2. Reprinted in *CP*:2.

39. Cooper, M. J., and M. M. Aygen. A relaxation technique in the management of hypercholesterolemia. *Journal of Human Stress* 5 (1979):24-27. Reprinted in *CP*:2.

40. Zamarra, J. W., I. Besseghini, and S. Wittenberg. The effects of the Transcendental Meditation program on the exercise performance of patients with angina pectoris. In *CP*:1.

41. Hornsberger, R. W., and A. F. Wilson. Transcendental Meditation in treating asthma. *Respiration Therapy: The Journal of Inhalation Technology* 3 (1973):79-80. Reprinted in *CP*:1.

42. Wilson, A. F., R. Hornsberger, J. T. Chiu, and H. S. Novey. Transcendental Meditation and asthma. *Respiration* 32 (1975):74-80. Reprinted in *CP*:1.

43. Fuson, J. W. The effect of the Transcendental Meditation program on sleeping and dreaming patterns. Doctoral dissertation, Yale Medical School, 1976. Summary in *CP*:2.

44. Wallace, R. K., M. C. Dillbeck, E. Jacobe, and B. Harrington. The effects of the Transcendental Meditation and TM-Sidhi program on the aging process. *International Journal of Neuroscience* 16 (1982):53-59.

45. Pirot, M. The effects of the Transcendental Meditation technique upon auditory discrimination. In *CP*:1.

46. Schwartz, E. The effects of the Transcendental Meditation program on strength of the nervous system, perceptual reactance, reaction time, and auditory threshold. Master's thesis, University of Massachusetts, 1979. Reprinted in *CP*:2.

47. Dillbeck, M. C. The effects of Transcendental Meditation technique on visual perception and verbal problem solving. *Memory and Cognition* 10 (1982):207-215.

48. Martinetti, R. F. Influence of Transcendental Meditation on perceptual illusion. *Perceptual and Motor Skills* 43 (1976):822. Reprinted in *CP*:2.

49. Pelletier, K. R. Influence of Transcendental Meditation upon autokinetic perception. *Perceptual and Motor Skills* 39 (1974):1031-1034. Reprinted in *CP*:1.

50. Shecter, H. W. A psychological investigation into the source of the effect of the Transcendental Meditation technique. Doctoral dissertation, York University, Toronto, 1978. Summary in *CP*:1.

51. Travis, F. The Transcendental Meditation technique and creativity: A longitudinal study of Cornell University undergraduates. *Journal of Creative Behavior* 13 (1979):169-180. Reprinted in *CP*:2.

52. Aron, A., D. W. Orme-Johnson, and P. Brubaker. The Transcendental Meditation program in the college curriculum: A four-year longitudinal study of effects on cognitive and affective functioning. *College Student Journal* 15 (1981):40-46.

53. Tjoa, A. S. Meditation, neuroticism, and intelligence: A follow-up. *Gedrag: Tijdschrift voor Psychologie* 3 (1975):167-182. Reprinted in *CP*:1.

54. Heaton, D. P., and D. W. Orme-Johnson. The Transcendental Meditation program and academic attainment. In *CP*:1.

55. Nidich, S. I. A study of the relationship of Transcendental Meditation to Kohlberg's stages of moral reasoning. Doctoral dissertation, University of Cincinnati. Summary in *CP*:1.

56. Abrams, A. I. The effects of meditation on elementary school students. Doctoral dissertation, University of California, 1976. Reprinted in *CP*:2.

57. Dillbeck, M. C. The effect of the Transcendental Meditation technique on anxiety level. *Journal of Clinical Psychology* 33 (1977):1076-1078. Reprinted in *CP*:2.

58. Ferguson, P. C., and J. C. Gowan. TM: Some preliminary findings. *Journal of Humanistic Psychology* 16 (1976):51-60. Reprinted in *CP*:1.

59. Hjelle, L. A. Transcendental Meditation and psychological health. *Perceptual and Motor Skills* 39 (1974):623-628. Reprinted in *CP*:1.

60. Wampler, L. D. TM and assertiveness training in the treatment of social anxiety. Doctoral dissertation, Vanderbilt University, 1978.

61. Zuroff, D. C., and J. C. Schwartz. Effects of Transcendental Meditation and muscle relaxation on trait anxiety, maladjustment, locus of control, and drug use. *Journal of Consulting and Clinical Psychology* 46 (1978):264-271.

62. Shapiro, J. S. The relationship of selected characteristics of Transcendental Meditation to measures of self-actualization, negative person-

ality characteristics, and anxiety. Doctoral Dissertation, University of Southern California, 1975. Summary in *CP*:1.
63. van den Berg, W. P., and B. Mulder. Psychological research on the effects of the Transcendental Meditation technique on a number of personality variables. *Gedrag: Tijdschrift voor Psychologie* 4 (1976):206-218. Reprinted in *CP*:1.
64. Nystul, M. S., and M. Garde. Comparison of self-concepts of Transcendental Meditators and nonmeditators. *Psychological Reports* 41 (1977):303-306. Reprinted in *CP*:2.
65. Willis, C. L. R. Transcendental Meditation and its influence on the self-concept. Doctoral dissertation, Texas A & M University, 1974. Summary in *CP*:2.
66. Kukulan, J., A. Aron, and A. I. Abrams. The Transcendental Meditation program and children's personality. In *CP*:3.
67. Nidich, S., W. Seeman, and T. Dreskin. Transcendental Meditation: A replication. *Journal of Counseling Psychology* 20 (1973):565-566. Reprinted in *CP*:1.
68. Russie, R. The influence of Transcendental Meditation on positive mental health and self-actualization, and the role of expectation, rigidity, and self-control in the achievement of these results. Doctoral dissertation, California School of Professional Psychology, Los Angeles, 1975. Summary in *CP*:2.
69. Scott, L. J. Transcendental Meditation: Effect on pre-treatment personality and prognostic subjects' self-actualizing changes while practicing Transcendental Meditation. Doctoral dissertation, Radford University, Radford, Virginia, 1978. Summary in *CP*:2.
70. Seeman, W., S. Nidich, and T. Banta. Influence of Transcendental Meditation on a measure of self-actualization. *Journal of Counseling Psychology* 19 (1972):184-187. Reprinted in *CP*:1.
71. Dick, L. D. A study of meditation in the service of counseling. Doctoral dissertation, University of Oklahoma, 1974. Summary in *CP*:1.
72. Glueck, B. C., and C. F. Stroebel. Biofeedback and meditation in the treatment of psychiatric illness. *Comprehensive Psychiatry* 16 (1975):303-321.
73. Aron, A., and E. N. Aron. The Transcendental Meditation program's effect on addictive behavior. *Addictive Behaviors* 5 (1980):3-12. Reprinted in *CP*:3.
74. Siegel, L. M. The Transcendental Meditation program and the treatment of drug abuse. In *Substance Abuse in the United States: Problems and Perspectives*. ed. J. H. Lowinson and P. Ruiz. Baltimore: Williams & Wilkins, 1981.

75. Aron, A., and E. N. Aron. Rehabilitation, community crime prevention and the Transcendental Meditation program. Paper presented at the Academy of Criminal Justice Sciences Annual Meeting, Louisville, Kentucky, March, 1982.
76. Orme-Johnson, D. W. Prison rehabilitation and crime prevention through the Transcendental Meditation and TM-Sidhi program. In *Holistic Approaches to Offender Rehabilitation,* ed. L. J. Hippchen, Springfield, Illinois: Charles C. Thomas, 1980.
77. Griggs, S. T. A preliminary study into the effect of Transcendental Meditation on empathy. Doctoral dissertation, United States International University, San Diego, 1976.
78. Aron, E. N., and A. Aron. Transcendental Meditation program and marital adjustment. *Psychological Reports* 51 (1982):887-890. Reprinted in *CP*:2.
79. Suarez, V. M. The relationship of the practice of Transcendental Meditation to subjective evaluations of marital satisfaction and adjustment. Master's thesis, University of Southern California, Los Angeles, 1976. Summary in *CP*:2.
80. Frew, D. R. Transcendental Meditation and productivity. *Academy of Management Journal* 17 (1974):362-368. Reprinted in *CP*:1.
81. Friend, K. E. Effects of the Transcendental Meditation program on work attitudes and behavior. In *CP*:1.
82. Orme-Johnson, D. W., R. K. Wallace, M. D. Dillbeck, O. Ball, and C. N. Alexander. Behavioral correlates of EEG phase coherence. Paper presented at the Annual Convention of the American Psychological Association, Los Angeles, August, 1981.
83. Dillbeck, M. C., D. W. Orme-Johnson, and R. K. Wallace. Frontal EEG coherence, H-reflex recovery, concept learning, and the TM-Sidhi program. *International Journal of Neuroscience* 15 (1981):151-157.
84. Aron, A., and E. Aron. The Transcendental Meditation program, higher states of consciousness, and supernormal abilities. Paper presented at the annual convention of the American Psychological Association, Toronto, August, 1978.
85. Dillbeck, M. C., A. P. Aron, and S. L. Dillbeck. The Transcendental Meditation program as an educational technology: Research and applications. *Educational Technology* 19 (1979):7-13.
86. Shear, J., and K. Eppley. Factors influencing the effectiveness of meditation and relaxation techniques. Paper presented at the Annual Convention of the American Psychological Association, Toronto, August 1984.

87. Selye, H. Foreword to *TM: Discovering Inner Energy and Overcoming Stress*, ed. H. H. Bloomfield, M. P. Cain, and D. T. Jaffee. New York: Delacorte, 1975, ix-xii.
88. Maslow, A. H. New introduction: Religious values in peak experiences. *Journal of Transpersonal Psychology* 2 (1970).
89. Banquet, J. P., and M. Sailhan. Quantified spectral analysis of sleep and Transcendental Meditation. Paper presented at the Second European Congress on Sleep Research, Rome, April, 1984. Reprinted in *CP*:1.
90. *Creating an Ideal Society*. Rheinweiler, West Germany: MERU Press, 1976.
91. Sperry, R. A modified concept of consciousness. *Psychological Review* 76 (1969):532-536.

CHAPTER 3

1. Wolters, C., ed. *The Cloud of Unknowing and Other Works*. New York: Penguin, 1978.
2. St. John of the Cross. *The Collected Works of St. John of the Cross*. Washington, DC: ICS Publications, 1979.
3. Schatz, R. The state of nothingness and contemplative prayer in Hasidism. In *Zen and Hasidism*, ed. H. Heifetz. Wheaton, IL: Quest, 1978.
4. Teshima, J. Y. Self-extinction in Zen and Hasidism. In *Zen and Hasidism*, ed. H. Heifetz. Wheaton, IL: Quest, 1978.
5. Borland, C., and G. Landrith. Improved quality of city life through the Transcendental Meditation program: Decreased crime rate. In *CP*:1.
6. Dillbeck, M. C., G. Landrith, and D. W. Orme-Johnson. The Transcendental Meditation program and crime rate change in a sample of 48 cities. *Journal of Crime and Justice* 4 (1981):24-25. Reprinted in *CP*:4.
7. Landrith, G. S., and M. C. Dillbeck. The growth of coherence in society through the Maharishi Effect: Reduced rates of suicides and auto accidents. In *CP*:4.
8. Hatchard, G. Influence of the Transcendental Meditation program on crime rate in suburban Cleveland. In *CP*:2.
9. Dillbeck, M. C., T. W. Bauer, and S. I. Vida. A compound probability model and the Transcendental Meditation program as predictors of crime rate change. Paper presented at the Midwest Sociological Society Meeting, Omaha, NE, 1978. Reprinted in *CP*:2.

10. Orme-Johnson, D. W., and M. C. Dillbeck. World peace proposal: A proposal to increase national coherence and to reduce violence in trouble-spot countries of the world. Unpublished paper, available from MIU, Fairfield, IA, 52556.
11. Dillbeck, M. C. Social field effects in crime prevention. Paper presented at the annual convention of the American Psychological Association, Los Angeles, 1981. (These data are included in the reference below.)
12. Dillbeck, M. C., G. S. Landrith, C. Polanzi and S. R. Baker. The Transcendental Meditation program and crime rate change: A causal analysis. In *CP*:4.

CHAPTER 4

1. Aranya, S. H. *Yoga Philosophy of Patanjali*. Calcutta: Pooran Press, 1963.
2. Orme-Johnson, D. W., R. K. Wallacle, M. C. Dillbeck, O. Ball, and C. N. Alexander. Behavioral correlates of EEG phase coherence. Paper presented at the Annual Convention of the American Psychological Association, Los Angeles, August, 1981. Reprinted in *CP*:2.
3. Zimmerman, W. J. Improved quality of life during the Rhode Island Ideal Society Campaign, Phase I, June 12, 1978 to September 12, 1978. Unpublished report, available from MIU, Fairfield, IA 52556.
4. Dillbeck, M. C., A. P. O. Foss, and W. J. Zimmerman. Maharishi's Global Ideal Society Campaign: Improved quality of life in Rhode Island through the Transcendental Meditation and TM-Sidhi program. In *CP*:4.

CHAPTER 5

1. Hobson, A. *Physics and Human Affairs*. New York: Wiley, 1982.
2. Josephson, B. Letter. *New Scientist* 82 (1979):940.
3. Domash, L. Introduction. In *CP*:1.
4. Hagelin, J. S. A unified understanding of natural law through the discovery of super-gravity. Paper presented at the International Symposium on the Applications of Modern Science and Natural Law. Kirchberg, Luxembourg, March 1982.
5. Sudarshan, E. C. G. Presentation on consciousness and the structure of the physical universe. International Conference on the Psychophysiology of the Siddhis. Weggis, Switzerland, May, 1977.
6. Einstein, A. *On the Method of Theoretical Physics*. New York: Oxford

University Press, 1933.
7. Pagels, H. *The Cosmic Code: Quantum Physics as the Language of Nature.* New York: Simon & Schuster, 1982.
8. Bohm, D. *Wholeness and the Implicate Order.* London: Routledge & Kegan Paul, 1980.
9. Capra, F. *The Tao of Physics.* Boulder: Shambhala, 1975.
10. Jung, C. G. Aion: Researches into the phenomenology of the self. In *Collected Works,* vol. 9. New York: Pantheon, 1959.
11. Jung, C. G. Mysterium conjiunctionis: An inquiry into the separation and synthesis of psychic opposites in alchemy. In *Collected Works* (Vol. 14, 2nd ed.). Princeton, NJ: Princeton University Press, 1970.
12. Sheldrake, R. *A New Science of Life: The Hypothesis of Formative Causation.* Los Angeles: Tarcher, 1981.

CHAPTER 6

1. *World Government News* 10 (October 1978).
2. *World Government News* 11 (Nov/Dec. 1978).
3. Maharishi Mahesh Yogi. Quoted by L. Domash in university-wide presidential address, Maharishi International University, October 21, 1978.
4. Orme-Johnson, D. W. Proposal to reduce violence in trouble spot countries of the world. *Peace Research Abstracts Journal* (1981).
5. Orme-Johnson, D. W., M. C. Dillbeck, and J. B. Bousquet. The World Peace Project of 1978: An experimental analysis of achieving world peace through the Maharishi Technology of the Unified Field. In *CP:*4.
6. Quoted by Orme-Johnson. The World Peace Project: An experimental analysis of achieving peace through the TM-Sidhi program. Unpublished manuscript, Maharishi International University, Fairfield, IA, 1979 (A later version of this paper appears in *CP:*4).
7. Azar, E. *Conflict and peace data bank (COPDAB): A computer-assisted approach to monitoring and analyzing international events.* Chapel Hill, N.C.: University of North Carolina at Chapel Hill, 1980.

CHAPTER 7

1. Burgmans, W. H. P. M., A. T. van der Burgt, F. P. Th. Lagenkamp, and B. A. Verstegen. Sociological effects of the groups dynamics of consciousness: Decrease of crime and traffic accidents in Holland. In *CP:*4.

2. Dillbeck, M. C., K. L. Cavanaugh, and W. P. van den Berg. The effect of the group dynamics of consciousness on society: Reduced crime in the Union Territory of Delhi, India. In *CP*:4.
3. Dillbeck, M. D., V. Mittlefehldt., A. P. Lukenbach, D. Childress, A. Royer, L. Westsmith, and D. W. Orme-Johnson. A time series analysis of the relationship between the group practice of the Transcendental Meditation and TM-Sidhi program and crime rate change in Puerto Rico. In *CP*:4.

CHAPTER 8

1. Orme-Johnson, D. W., C. N. Alexander, J. L. Davies, H. M. Chandler, and W. E. Larimore. International peace project in the Middle East: The effect of the Maharishi Technology of the Unified Field. In *CP*:4.
2. Lanford, A. G. Reduction in homicide in Washington, D. C. through the Maharishi Technology of the Unified Field, 1980-1983: A time series analysis. In *CP*:4.
3. Lanford, A. G. The effect of the Maharishi Technology of the Unified Field on stock prices of Washington, D. C. area-based corporations, 1980-1983: A time series analysis. In *CP*:4.
4. U. S. Federal Bureau of Investigation (1982). *Unified Crime Reports: Crime in the U. S.*. Washington, D.C.: U. S. Department of Justice.
5. Aron, A., & E. N. Aron. Evidence from Transcendental Meditation research for a social field. In *General Systems Research and Design: Precursors and Futures*. Edited by W. J. Reckmeyer. Louisville: Society for General Systems Research, 1981.
6. Aron, A., & E. N. Aron. *Experimental interventions of high coherence groups into disorderly social systems*. Paper presented at the annual convention of the American Psychological Association, Los Angeles, 1981.
7. Orme-Johnson, D. W., M. S. Dillbeck, R. K. Wallace, & G. Landrith. Intersubject EEG coherence: Is consciousness a field? *International Journal of Neuroscience 16* (1982): 203-209. Reprinted in *CP*:2.

CHAPTER 9

1. Aron, A., D. W. Orme-Johnson, and P. Brubaker. The Transcendental Meditation program in the college curriculum: A four-year longitudinal study of effects on cognitive and affective functioning. College Student Journal 15 (1981):40-46.
2. Dillbeck, M. C., W. E. Larimore, and R. K. Wallace. A time series

analysis of the effect of the Maharishi Technology of the Unified Field: Reduction of traffic fatalities in the United States. In *CP*:4.
3. Orme-Johnson, D. W., and P. Gelderloos. The long term effects of the Maharishi Technology of the Unified Field on the quality of life in the United States (1960 to 1983). In *CP*:4.
4. M.I.U. Influence of the group dynamics of consciousness on the stock market and on national and international events and trends. In *Maharishi International University 1983-1984*. Fairfield, IA: MIU Press, 1983.
5. Davies, J. L., and C. N. Alexander. The Maharishi Technology of the Unified Field and improved quality of life in the United States: A study of the First World Peace Assembly, Amherst, Massachusetts, 1979. In *CP*:4.
6. Cavanaugh, K. L., D. W. Orme-Johnson, and P. Gelderloos. The effect of the Taste of Utopia Assembly on the World Index of international stock prices. In *CP*:4.
7. Orme-Johnson, D. W., K. L. Cavanaugh, C. N. Alexander, P. Gelderloos, M. Dillbeck, A. G. Lanford, and T. M. Abou Nader. The influence of the Maharishi Technology of the Unified Field on world events and global social indicators: The effects of the Taste of Utopia Assembly. In *CP*:4.

CHAPTER 10

1. Aron, E. N., and A. Aron. Psychology's progress and the psychologist's personal experience. *The Journal of Mind and Behavior* 2 (1981):397-406.
2. Raye, R. H., and R. A. Arthur. Life change and illness studies. *Journal of Human Stress* 4 (1978):3-15.
3. Abrams, A. I. The effects of meditation on elementary school students. Doctoral Dissertation, University of California, 1976. Summary in *CP*:2.
4. Alexander, C., E. Langer, R. Neuman, H. Chandler, and J. Davies. TM and mindfulness: an experimental intervention study with the institutionalized elderly. Unpublished manuscript, Harvard University Department of Psychology and Social Relations, 1983.
5. Daniels, D. Comparison of the Transcendental Meditation technique to various relaxation procedures. In *CP*:2.
6. Glueck, B. C. and C. F. Stroebel. Physiological correlates of relaxation. In *Expanding Dimensions of Consciousness*, ed. Sugarman, A. A. and R. E. Tarter. New York: Springer Publishing, 1977.

7. Lewis, R. In *Happiness: The TM Program, Psychiatry, and Enlightenment*, Bloomfield, H. and R. Kory. New York: Dawn Press/Simon and Schuster, 1974.
8. Morse, D., J. Martin, M. Furst and L. Dubin. A physiological and subjective evaluation of meditation, hypnosis, and relaxation. *Psychosomatic Medicine* 39 (1977): 304-324.
9. Riddle, A. Effects of selected elements of meditation on self-actualization, locus of control, and trait anxiety. Doctoral Dissertation, University of South Carolina, 1979.
10. Rosenthal, J. M. The effect of the Transcendental Meditation program on self-actualization, self-concept, and hypnotic susceptibility. Masters' thesis, University of Hawaii, 1974. Summary in *CP*:2.
11. Tolliver, D. Personality as a factor determining response to two different meditation techniques. Senior thesis, Princeton University, 1976. In *Freedom to Meditation*, Carrington, P. New York: Anchor Press/Doubleday, 1977.
12. Shear, J. and K. Eppley. *Factors Influencing the Effectiveness of Meditation and Relaxation Techniques.* Paper presented at the Annual Convention of the American Psychological Association, Toronto, August 1984.
13. Maslow, A. H. *The Farther Reaches of Human Nature.* New York: Penguin, 1971.
14. Alexander, C. N. Transcendental Meditation effects on ego development and personality validated in prisoners. Paper presented at the annual convention of the American Psychological Association, Los Angeles, August 1981.
15. Nidich, S. I. A study of the relationship of Transcendental Meditation to Kohlberg's stages of moral reasoning. Doctoral Dissertation, University of Cincinnati, 1976. Summary in *CP*:1.
16. Orme-Johnson, D. W., R. K. Wallace, M. C. Dillbeck, O. Ball, and C. N. Alexander. Behavorial correlates of EEG phase coherence. Paper presented at the Annual Convention of the American Psychological Association, Los Angeles, August 1981.

INDEX

Academic performance, 10
Air-traffic accidents, 143, 146, 156
Alcohol consumption, 64, 66, 141
Alexander, C. ("Skip"), 121, 123, 126, 127, 143
Amherst, MA, 131, 132, 136, 143
Archetypes, 84
Augustine, St., 4, 18
Auto accidents, 63, 66, 116, 118, 124, 141, 143, 149
Ba'al Shem Tov, 40
Baer, Rabbi Dov, 40
Banquet, J.-P., 30
Bauer, T., 50
Borland, C., 43
Brain waves, see EEG coherence
Brett, G., 4, 5
Bucke, R., 18
Buddhism, 4, 41, 81
Capra, F., 80
Cavanaugh, K., 119
Central America, see Nicaragua
Christianity, 4, 30, 39, 81
Cigarette sales, 65, 66, 141
Cleveland, OH, 50
Cloud of Unknowing, 39
Collective consciousness, 74, 80
Collective unconscious, 84, 85
Conflict and Peace Data Bank (COPDAB), 106, 107
Consciousness
  Coherence in, 72
  Definition of, 31
  Higher states of, 29–33

Crime rate, 16, 35, 43, 51, 62–64, 66, 116, 118–120, 128–129, 140, 143, 149, 156
Cross-lagged panel analysis, 51
Davies, J. L., 143
D. C. (Washington, D. C.), 16, 127–130, 132, 157, 159
de Chardin, T., 155
Death rate, 63, 66, 124, 141, 143
Delhi, India, 16, 113, 118–119
Dillbeck, M., 47, 48–51, 65, 119
Domash, L., 80
EEG coherence, 3, 22, 31–33, 42, 53, 58–59, 132
Einstein, A., 11, 75
Fairfield, IA, 60, 132, 135–138, 144, 159
Farrow, J., 21, 22, 25
Fechner, G., 18
Field, 41, 73–88
  Of consciousness, 73–88
  In physics, 72
  Unified, 11, 15, 77–83, 158
Fires, 124, 126
Foss, A., 65
Freud, S., 4, 84
Fuller, B., 155
Group dynamics of consciousness, 112
Hagelin, J., 80
Hasidism, see Judaism
Hatchard, G., 50
Holland, 16, 113, 115–118, 126
Homicide, 62–63, 120, 128–129
Index of National Progress, 123
Infectious diseases, 149
Iowa, see Fairfield, IA

Iran, 1-3, 16, 92, 95-96
Isaac, Rabbi Levi, 40
Israel, 16, 92, 99-100, 121-127, 130, 132
John of the Cross, St., 40
Josephson, B., 72
Judaism, 4, 40, 81
Jung, C., 11, 18, 74, 84-86
Kansas City, 50
Landrith, G., 10, 43, 45, 48-50
Lanford, A., 128-130
Lebanon, 122, 124
Longevity, 10
Maharishi Effect formula, 112, 120, 122
Maharishi International University, 135-138
Maharishi Mahesh Yogi, 7, 42, 58
Maharishi's Technology of the Unified Field, 113
Marriage and divorce, 10, 62, 66, 141, 156
Maslow, A., 30, 159
Moral judgment, 10
Morphogenetic field, 84, 86-88
Natural law, 81
Nicaragua, 92, 94-95, 110
One-percent effect, 44, 47-49, 52
One-percent studies, 43-44, 113-120
Orme-Johnson, D., 10, 50, 93, 101-102, 106, 123, 126-127, 131
Patanjali, 5, 57-59
Patent applications, 149
Peace, 91-108, 123, 139
Phase transitions, 39, 41-43
Philo, 4
Plato, 4, 11
Plotinus, 4
Pollution, 65-66, 156
Productivity, 140-141
Puerto Rico, 16, 113, 119-120

Quality of life index, 60
Quantum field theory, 11, 70-83
Quantum physics, see Quantum field theory
Rhode Island, 16, 55-67, 91, 110, 114, 126
Rhodesia (Zimbabwe), see Southern Africa
Russell, P., 155
Samadhi, 4, 5
Selye, H., 10, 28
Seven thousand, 16, 133, 144-145, 151, 156-158
Sheldrake, R., 77, 84, 86-88
Sioux, 5
Social incoherence, 3
Southeast Asia, 92, 100-101, 110
Southern Africa, 92, 96-99
Sperry, R., 31
Stock market, 124, 126, 129-130, 138-139, 141, 144
Stress, 10, 26-28, 35
Sudarshan, G., 80
Suicide, 62, 143, 156
Superradiance, 112
Tehran, see Iran
Teresa of Avila, St., 5, 18
Teshima, J., 40
Thailand, see Southeast Asia
Time series analysis, 65-67, 114-115, 120, 123, 125-128, 130, 149
Transcendental Meditation (TM) technique, 7-9, 18-28, 43-45, 136, 159
  Research on, 19-34
  Teachers of, 56-57
TM-Sidhi techniques, 47, 58, 81-82, 92, 111, 124, 138
Unconscious, 84
Unemployment, 64-66, 142
Unified field, see Field, Unified
van Den Berg, W., 119
Veda, 30, 42, 80-81

Index

Vida, S., 50
Violence, see Crime rate, Homicide, Peace
Wallace, R., 9–10, 27
War, see Peace
Washington, D. C., see D. C.
Weather, 65, 125–126, 142, 144
World Peace Assemblies, 113
World Peace Project, 92–108, 110, 113, 157
Yoga Sutras, 57
Zambia, see Southern Africa
Zen, 9, 41
Zimmerman, W., 60, 65

STILLPOINT PUBLISHING

Books that explore the expanding frontiers of human consciousness

For a free catalog or ordering information

write:

Stillpoint Publishing
Box 640, Walpole, NH 03608 USA

or call

1-800-847-4014 TOLL FREE
(Continental US, except NH)

1-603-756-4225 or 756-3508
(Foreign and NH)